Spirituality in History Series

The Benedictine Tradition

Laura Swan, Editor

Phyllis Zagano, Series Editor

LITURGICAL PRESS
Collegeville, Minnesota

www.litpress.org

Cover design by Ann Blattner. Cover art: *Saint Benedict,* fresco painting from the Abbey at Monte Cassino, Italy, XIV.

1 2 3 4 5 6 7 8 9

Library of Congress Cataloging-in-Publication Data

Swan, Laura, 1954–
The Benedictine tradition / Laura Swan, Phyllis Zagano.
p. cm. — (Spirituality in history series)
Includes bibliographical references.
ISBN 978-0-8146-1914-8
1. Benedictines—Spiritual life. I. Zagano, Phyllis. II. Title.

BX3003.S93 2007
271'.1—dc22

2007000761

Contents

Acknowledgments

Excerpt from *Gregory the Great: The Life of Saint Benedict*. Translated by Hilary Costello and Eoin de Bhaldraithe. Commentary by Adalbert de Vogüé. Petersham, MA: St. Bede's Publications, 1993. Used with permission.

Excerpt from Bede the Venerable's *Homilies on the Gospels: Book Two—Lent to the Dedication of the Church*. Translated by Lawrence T. Martin and David Hurst. Kalamazoo, MI: Cistercian Publications, 1991. Used with permission.

Excerpt from Peter Damian's *Life of St. Romuald of Ravenna*, in *Medieval Hagiography: an Anthology*. Edited by Thomas Head and Translated by Henrietta Leyser. Copyright 2000. Reproduced by permission of Routledge/Taylor & Francis Group, LLC.

Excerpt from *St. Anselm ~ Proslogium; Monologium; an Appendix in Behalf of the Fool by Gaunilon; and Cur Deus Homo*. Translated by Sidney Norton Deane. Chicago: Open Court Publishing, 1903. Public Domain.

Excerpt from Hildegard of Bingen's *Scivias* is from *Secrets of God* © 1996 by Sabina Flanagan. Reprinted by arrangement with Shambhala Publications, Inc., Boston, www.shambhala.com.

Reproduced from Hildegard of Bingen: *Symphonia: a Critical Edition of the "Symphonia Armonie Celestium Revelationuma; (Symphony of the Harmony of Celestial Revelations)*, Second Edition edited and translated by Barbara Newman. Copyright © 1988, 1998 by Cornell University. Used with permission of the publisher, Cornell University Press.

Excerpt from Bernard of Clairvaux, *Sermon 74 on the Song of Songs*. Translated by Michael Casey, o.s.c.o., 1990. Used with permission of the translator.

Excerpt from *Gertrud the Great: The Herald of God's Loving-Kindness—Books 1 and 2*. Translated by Alexandra Barratt. Kalamazoo, MI: Cistercian Publications, 1991. Used with permission.

Excerpt from *Augustine Baker,* O.S.B., *The Life and Death of Dame Gertrude More* edited from all the known manuscripts by Ben Wekking. Salzburg, Austria: Analecta Cartusiana, 2002. Permission for use granted by publisher.

Extract from *Christ, the Life of the Soul: Spiritual Conferences by Blessed Columba Marmion,* O.S.B., newly translated by Alan Bancroft, copyright Zaccheus Press, Maryland (zaccheuspress.com) and Gracewing Publishing, 2005 and used with permission.

I have made every effort to locate the current copyright holder for *We Have Always Been Friends Together* and *Adventures in Grace: the Memoirs of Raïssa Maritain*, originally published by Magi Books. Acknowledgment will be made in future editions if the copyright holder contacts this publisher.

The Golden String: an Autobiography by Bede Griffiths, Templegate Publishers (templegate.com), 1954, 1980. *A New Vision of Reality: Western Science, Eastern Mysticism and Christian Faith*, by Bede Griffiths, Templegate Publishers (templegate.com) 1989. Used with permission.

Excerpts from Bernardo Olivera's *How Far to Follow? The Martyrs of Atlas*. Petersham, MA: St. Bede Publications, 1997. Used with permission.

Excerpts from the Conference of Benedictine Prioresses *Wisdom from the Tradition: A Statement of North American Benedictine Women in Response to Our Times*. Copyright 2006, Conference of Benedictine Prioresses. Used with permission.

Quotes from RB (Rule of Benedict) are from *Benedict's Rule: a Translation and Commentary* by Terrence Kardong, O.S.B. Copyright 1996, Liturgical Press.

Preface

The worldwide explosion of interest in "spirituality" has sent inquirers in several directions. One of the more fruitful is toward the traditional spiritualities that have enriched and nurtured the church for many hundreds of years. Among the oldest Christian spiritualities are those connected to particular foundations, charisms, or individuals. This series of spiritualities in history focuses on five distinct traditions within the history of the church, those now known as Benedictine, Carmelite, Dominican, Franciscan, and Ignatian.

Each volume in this series seeks to present the given spiritual tradition through an anthology of writings by or about persons who have lived it, along with brief biographical introductions of those persons. Each volume is edited by an expert in the tradition at hand. Each can serve as the foundation of a course in the given tradition, or as a guide for personal reading.

The present volume of Benedictine spirituality has been edited by Laura Swan, O.S.B., former prioress of St. Placid Priory in Lacey, Washington, and author of three other books on spirituality, whose breadth and depth of knowledge of her tradition has allowed her to draw together the boldest threads from the tapestry of Benedictine history and present them in a manner accessible to all.

This book presents but a taste of the deep and rich spirituality of the followers of Saint Benedict, and is offered in recognition of his and their magnificent contributions to the church in the fifteen centuries since he first joined monastics together in community. The lives and writings of the Benedictine men and women in this volume show how remarkable and dedicated Benedictines have continued to be faithful to St. Benedict's and St. Scholastica's vision as monastics devoted to the prayer of the church. Each entry shows a different facet of the crystallized spirituality of St. Benedict, chosen from among the thousands of Benedictine men and women who have lived that spirituality over the centuries. Those included present only a snapshot of the whole, without the rich detail that many volumes could present.

My own work on this book and for this series has continued with the able assistance of librarians, particularly the reference and interlibrary loan staff at Hofstra University, Hempstead, New York, and the library staff at Marymount College, Tarrytown, New York, especially Mary Elizabeth Rathgeb, R.S.H.M. For his support and encouragement with this project I am most grateful to Peter Dwyer, Director of Liturgical Press.

Phyllis Zagano
January 15, 2007
Feast of Sts. Maurus and Placid

Introduction

We live in a world undergoing change at a breathtaking pace. Our economy and politics have become intertwined through globalization, and the powerful have prevailed and profited. We are challenged by heart-wrenching injustice; genocide is common and familiar. We are busy and disconnected from one another. Isolation and addiction siege our souls. Our willingness to accept illusion and façade, shattered families, mobility and pseudo-intimacy through technology have left us wondering who we are and how we are to be in this alien world. Something from the ancient past and from the desert calls to our parched hearts, impelling us to look anew. There is a better way to live and relate and create.

Benedictine spirituality is enjoying a renaissance. The simplicity of St. Benedict's way, the humble wisdom that abides in his spiritual teachings, and his ardent desire to help all seekers succeed in the spiritual journey entices even the most reticent to hearken to his words. St. Benedict gifted the church with his "modest Rule for beginners" (RB 73:8), instructions for a monastic way of life. Today people are integrating the Benedictine values of hospitality, stability, work, and prayer both inside and outside the monastery to deepen the meaning in their lives and draw near to God.

Grounded in Benedict's Rule, Benedictine spirituality is the wisdom resulting from fifteen hundred years of wrestling with the meaning and practicalities of living Benedict's teaching in everyday life. It is the written and oral heritage of many generations and cultures pondering and reflecting on the Rule. With Benedictine monasteries established in many cultures and most nations, Benedictine spirituality is finding diverse expression while maintaining continuity. Benedictine spirituality engages that tradition with contemporary society and other religious and monastic traditions. We seek wisdom from the past and guidance for making life choices in our turbulent times. Our souls know: there must be a better way.

The twins Benedict (480–550) and Scholastica (480–547) demonstrate for us healthy relationships—with one another and with God—which are the foundation of community life. Seeking God together in community evokes a response of reverent prayer and compassionate ministry. While the twins had no sense that they were establishing a religious order that would literally transverse the ends of the earth, their simple obedience to the Holy Spirit broadened their hearts and showed thousands the way to God through the monastic observance.

Venerable Bede, Monk of Jarrow (673–735), is one of Christianity's earliest historians, and a most gifted scholar. He observed some of the struggles as Roman Christianity confronted and engaged Celtic Christianity, each with its differing expressions of the liturgical life of the church. Bede was also a simple monk in love with God, and love of God is the core essence of the monastic journey.

Romuald of Ravenna (950–1027) craved silence and solitude yet fully understood the monastic journey as a corporate one—we are all connected in Christ and we journey together to Christ. His brilliance was to emphasize that aspect of the Rule of Benedict easily overlooked: that once the monastic has matured in cenobitic community, a life of solitude as a hermit may be the next stage of that monastic's life. He showed us how to meld the cenobitic (communal) and the eremitic, or hermit's way, while remaining one monastic community.

Anselm of Canterbury (1033–1109) was an exemplary monk and scholar who lived through a quiet intellectual renaissance within Christianity. He also lived through challenging times in regard to the relationship of church and state. A monk who would have preferred to be left alone in his monastic world, he found himself thrust into political turmoil not of his making. His humble obedience in accepting the office of Bishop of Canterbury showed us how to stand and defend the gospel from secular politicking.

A reformer's reformer, a powerful charismatic personality, a man never lacking in an opinion, Bernard of Clairvaux (1090–1153) truly loved God. His writings reveal a man ever in wonder of God's love for us, as well as a monk who desired that his readers savor this divine love.

We have witnessed a resurgence of interest in Abbess Hildegard of Bingen (1098–1179). She has been the subject of extensive scholarly research as well as popular works. Her music has been performed and is currently available on compact discs. Students of Hildegard have been examining her studies of science and medicine.

Gertrud the Great of Helfta (1256–1302) lived most of her life within the cloister of her monastery, a monastery rich in talented and uniquely gifted nuns. Besides sharing the rich tapestry of her interior life, Gertrud wrote a series of spiritual exercises for the benefit of her nuns and those who came to her for spiritual direction.

Dame Gertrude More (1606–1633) lived in an era of virulent persecution against Catholics in England. As with others wanting to live a religious life, she slipped out of England to the continent and, with a small group of like-minded women, began an English-speaking Benedictine monastery. Her writings, published posthumously, speak to our contemporary sensibility: she was a scrupulous perfectionist who came to trust her personal experience of God, and hers was a burning passion for God alone.

Blessed Columba Marmion (1858–1923) was a much loved and respected abbot who served his community during trying times: the German occupation of Belgium during the First World War and the establishment of a new Benedictine Congregation. His was an easy movement between the world of academia and everyday spirituality. Pope John Paul II acknowledged the importance of Marmion's writings to the history of Catholic spirituality and praised him for emphasizing the centrality of Christ.

Raïssa Maritain (1883–1940), along with her sister Vera and her husband Jacques, became Benedictine oblates. Their monastic community was in their shared home, complete with times for prayer and silence. Oblates, lay people who commit their lives to following Benedict's Rule as much as they are able, have long been a blessing and significant part of the Benedictine world. Selections from Raïssa's journal reveal a quiet and passionate mystic who remained firmly grounded in this world.

Bede Griffiths (1906–1993), is one example of the Benedictine commitment to East/West dialogue. In India, he established a Christian Ashram with fellow Benedictines. Here he came to learn from all his neighbors, primarily Hindu, and allow them to shape his heart and his search for God.

As with all serious seekers of the divine, there are Benedictine martyrs: those who witness to the possibility of something higher that is grounded in love. Seven Trappist Martyrs (d. 1996) knew that death was a possibility and a probability when they decided to stay with their neighbors who did not have the option of escaping the civil war destroying Algeria.

Selections from the letters of Brother Christian reveal a heart that embraces the possibility of death—for that is where the possibility of resurrection lay.

While chant did not begin with Benedictines, the preservation of the chant tradition even in the midst of innovations and differing cultural expressions has long been near and dear to the hearts of the Benedictine world. Pope Gregory the Great, Guido D'Arezzo, Abbess Hildegard, the Benedictines of Solesmes and the leaders of the twentieth-century liturgical movement were all dedicated to keeping chant, so essential to Benedictine liturgies, alive.

Monastic leadership continues its task of listening together and asking: how is the Holy Spirit calling us as Benedictines? There are never clear and simple answers; rather, wisdom emerges as we ponder together the concerns and joys of our hearts. The Conference of Benedictine Prioresses strive to give voice to their concerns and convictions in the midst of a dominant culture of violence: What might Benedict and Scholastica say to seekers today?

I want to give special thanks for input and assistance from series editor, Phyllis Zagano, Benedictine Sisters Mary Giles Mailhot, Dorothy Robinson, and Lucy Wynkoop as well as to Karen Barrueto, and Walter and Renata Siegl for all their assistance and support.

The Benedictine Tradition

The Benedictine Tradition has its origins in a relatively small text written in an obscure monastery south of Rome, somewhere between 530 and 550 C.E. Yet the Rule of Benedict is generally acknowledged as one of the most influential documents of Western Civilization. Its author, Benedict of Nursia (480–ca. 550), is a gentle genius of the monastic way of life.

The World of Saint Benedict

The twins, Benedict and Scholastica, lived fifteen hundred years ago in an era distant from our own. Yet in so many ways, the challenges of their day resonate with our own. They were born into an empire that was undergoing enormous social, economic, and political upheaval. The Roman Empire was dealing with massive movements of people: those wanting to enter the empire to seek opportunity as well as those wanting to leave to avoid excessive taxation and conscription into a deteriorating military. Disease and hunger were wiping out populations, leaving the farms abandoned. The birth rate for the upper class had dropped to an all-time low, due in part to a breakdown in the institution of marriage as well as abortion and infanticide. Civil war among the patrician families, fed by political corruption and greed, led to political insecurity. Crime was rampant.

Christianity, while slowly emerging as the prevalent religion of the Roman Empire, had been wracked by internal strife: was Jesus of Nazareth fully human and fully divine (the Orthodox position)? Was he somehow less divine and fully human (Arianism)? Was he fully divine and merely appeared human (Docetism)? Christianity had nearly been torn asunder with theological and political internal strife. Although the Nicene

Creed had been settled some years before Benedict and Scholastica were born, resolving some of the Christological controversies, namely Jesus of Nazareth as fully human and fully divine, rumbles of strife remained, especially concerning Arianism.

Christian monasticism essentially began in the desert and in the urban home churches. Oral and written traditions, commonly referred to as rules, were passed down and spread around the Roman Empire as monastic communities were sent into exile over the raging theological debates and through interference from a political system that feared further deterioration of the empire if the Christian community ever splintered. Benedict knew the rules of Pachomius in Egypt, Basil in the Eastern Empire, the Rule of the Four Fathers, Caesarius in Gaul and the unidentified author of the Rule of the Master.

For the simple men coming to Benedict for mentoring in the monastic life, these rules were far too long and complex. Most of his followers were barely converted and catechized, from differing tribes and cultures, and illiterate or barely able to read. Benedict's gentle genius was to take what was useful from these rules as well as from the writings of John Cassian, add some of his own thoughts, and create his "modest Rule for beginners" (RB 73:8).

The Rule of Benedict is known for its simplicity and balance. He took the essentials of the monastic way of life and concern for the interior, spiritual journey, recognized the humanity of his simple followers, and exhorted them to begin with his simple practices. When they had reached a level of maturity and yearned to strive for something harder, they could pick up one of the more strenuous rules, conferences and institutes, the church mothers and fathers and Sacred Scripture.

Benedict's genius extended further in that his Rule quietly undermined the corruption and degradation of his time. He demanded that his followers from the higher strata of society learn to do manual labor and that his illiterate monks learn to read. His monastery was to be a place of peace in the midst of civil war. The outcast, the sick, and the poor were to be received as Christ, and all of life was recognized as holy. His was a lay movement in an era of increasing clericalism. All his monks were to observe the monastic way equally. All were to be one in Christ.

The Benedictine Family

Sometime between 577 and 581, the Lombards destroyed the monastery at Monte Cassino and the surviving monks fled to their monastery of St. Pancratius, located at the Basilica of St. John Lateran in Rome. Pope St. Gregory the Great (540–604) most likely encountered these monks and heard the oral tradition of Benedict's life and possibly read a copy of his Rule at this community in Rome. From Gregory we received *Dialogues*, in which the hagiography surrounding Benedict's memory was fashioned to serve the pope's desire to inspire his flock to lives of greater holiness.

Benedict remained a virtual unknown. Monasteries continued to live according to their own traditions and rule, but increasingly they created "mixed rules" in which the Rule of Columbanus and the Rule of Benedict were the major influences. Monte Cassino, one of many monasteries in the Roman Empire, was restored in 717, but would face destruction repeatedly in its history.

Charlemagne (742–814) had pressed for conformity and uniformity regarding liturgical practices in the Catholic Church. He saw the church as the unifying force in an unwieldy and vast empire that was continually under threat of disintegration. Among his many "reforms" was his insistence that monasteries adopt the Rule of Benedict.

Benedict of Aniane (ca. 750–821) had been a member of Charlemagne's court and left to establish a monastery at Aniane in Languedoc. His initial attempts were rather austere and met with failure; he then adopted the Rule of Benedict and his monastic community flourished.

With Charlemagne's support, Benedict of Aniane pressed relentlessly for the monasteries of the empire to set aside the diversity of mixed rules and practices that had been the norm of their monasteries and adopt the Rule of Benedict. He stressed a rigidity and austerity not found in the Rule of Benedict. Benedict of Aniane also centralized authority and himself ruled all other abbots. While his "reforms" did not last much beyond his death, a movement began that would pave the way for true reform to occur in the next centuries.

Monasteries historically suffered from interference from rulers and royal families. Motives for establishing a royal monastery were always mixed: a desire to promote holiness, access to a place to retreat for prayer, schools for royal children, and stability in an unstable world. Too often royal monasteries were established to provide a suitable career for second and third offspring. Corruption seeped in and monastic practices often became lax; a secular ruler appointed abbots, and too often the office was sold to the highest bidder, with the abbot rarely in residence at the monastery.

Beginning with Cluny in 910, authentic reform swept the monastic world. Reformers sought to restore authentic Benedictine observance, liberate monasteries from secular influence (especially around freedom in electing abbots), and stabilize their economic security by returning ownership of monasteries to the collective monastic community. These first reform movements also sought to create an Order: rather than each monastery being autonomous, they would be grouped with a centralized authority. At Cluny, the abbot retained authority over all dependent houses, the latter being governed only by priors as his vicars. Cluny grew to an order of nearly 314 houses throughout Europe. General Chapters, gatherings of leadership from among the member monasteries, were called; here legal and economic business was conducted, homilies given, and the charism of the order perpetuated.

In 1098 another reform began at Cîteaux as a response to the elaborate lifestyle and liturgical practices that had grown at Cluny. Cîteaux, or "Cistercians" as these Benedictines would become known, sought to return to simplicity of lifestyle with an emphasis on the interior life. Cistercians became known as the Benedictines of the Strict Observance.

Some reform movements sought to stress the eremitical or hermit expression of Benedictine monasticism (Camaldoli in 1009); to reaffirm the value of double monasteries, which were especially prevalent in Great Britain (Fontevrault); and to establish monasteries as a response to local needs (Vallombrosa [1039], Grammont [1076], Savigny [1112], Monte Vergine [1119], Sylvestrines [1231], Celestines [1254], and Olivetans [1319]). Much later was a reform of the Cistercians called the Cistercians of the Strict Observance, or "Trappists."

Reforms, great and small, continued throughout the centuries. Systematic congregations were formed in compliance with the reforming decrees of the Council of Trent. Concerns included liturgical abuses, appropriate formation of monastics, and the need for Benedictines to connect with one another for mutual support and spiritual growth. These formal and informal connections proved valuable as different nations, in the midst of political turmoil, closed and evicted entire monastic communities.

Benedictine Spirituality

The Monastic Promise

Observe a Benedictine monk or nun as he or she enters the monastic chapel (or church). That monastic will bow to the altar before proceeding to his or her place in choir. Benedictines acknowledge the place where they have made their monastic profession: at the altar where each signed their profession document and where the relics of the saints are kept. Altars in the time of Benedict were the place that all Romans—Christian or not—made solemn oaths and/or swore on legal documents. Christians offered the holy sacrifice of Jesus' Body and Blood on the altar. Monasticism placed the whole life of the one making profession on the altar as an offering to God.

Benedictines make monastic profession, which encompasses stability, obedience, and faithfulness to the monastic way of life. Placing the signed document of profession on the altar reinforces the reality that the monastic has offered self to God completely. The monastic then chants the *suscipe*: "Receive me, O God, as you have promised, and I shall live; do not disappoint me in my hope" (RB 58:21). The monastic community, as a reminder of their own public offering of self to God and as a commitment to journey together with this new monastic, joins in chanting the *suscipe*.

Stability means that the monastic commits oneself to live out monastic life with a particular group of people in a particular monastery. Stability means that the monastic commits to persevere, day-by-day, through monotony and challenges and all the unknowns that life hands us. Stability supports the search for God.

Obedience is multifaceted. The monastic commits to live under the Rule and the superior. By implication, the monastic desires to live under the living tradition of this particular monastery. Obedience in the Rule is also mutual obedience, to listen to one another and to prefer the will of one another over one's own. Obedience is a commitment to daily discernment of how the Holy Spirit is calling us—a communal us as well as an individual us—each day and into the future.

Faithfulness to the monastic way of life or *conversatio morum suorum* is also translated conversion of life. This is a commitment to follow the monastic observances into a transformation of inner and outer self with a goal of purity of heart.

The evangelical vows of poverty, chastity, and obedience are a much later development with the rise of the Dominicans and Franciscans. However, Benedict clearly assumed poverty (radical inner and outer simplicity) and chastity (chaste celibacy) when a person came to the monastery seeking entrance. All vowed religious enter into a call from God to serve the people of God and to seek a deepened and mature relationship with God. Monastic profession serves to support that call to be a sign of God's presence in our midst.

The Common Life

Benedictines live in community. This is more than a physical reality; it is psychological and spiritual as well. In the common life, monastics seek God together. In the common life, the monastic allows the decisions of leadership, of the elders and *senpectae* (wise one), and of the weakest members to impact the individual monastic. In the common life, the monastic is committed to the very best for others.

Community discerns together choices for ministry direction, expenditures, work assignments, charities to support, corporate/political stands to take in the name of the community and much, much more. Common life means that each monastic will share his or her wisdom and then support the community decision, even when the particular monastic did not agree with it.

Common life is not based on natural friendships, although those often occur. Instead the monastic cultivates inclusive and intentional friendships with each member as a natural extension of life committed together in the monastery. Relationships are interdependent and mutual and empowering of one another. The common life shapes our hearts: the natural rubbing of edges, learning from one another, and the burden of bearing one another invites us to cultivate inner detachment and to find Christ in our fellow monastics. One of our modern ascetic practices is living well with one another. Who needs more?

The Divine Office and Prayer

Benedictines frame their day with times of public prayer and private prayer. Divine Office or Liturgy of the Hours may be celebrated two or three times daily, or upwards of seven times per day. Benedict advised his followers on how he recommended the day be framed (RB 8–20 and more) then encouraged his followers to do what they deem best for their communities. The point is not how monastic communities gather for the Divine Office, but that the community gathers daily with forethought and prayerful consideration. The Divine Office supports the communal and individual search for God. Like water slowly dropping on rock until that rock's shape has changed, the daily mundane task of chanting the Divine Office slowly works on an individual's heart, shaping the person into the image of Christ.

Benedictines also commit regular time for private prayer. *Lectio Divina* is the one form of prayer most closely associated with the tradition. In *lectio*, the monastic slowly savors a text, slowing when a word or phrase leaps out and touches the heart. After pondering prayerfully the phrase, the monastic continues on with the slow reading. *Lectio* is a heart reading of a text, not head. The monastic chews over a text much like a cow chews its cud. The goal is to soften and shape one's heart, not gain knowledge.

Traditionally Sacred Scripture has been the text savored in *lectio*. However, any text can feed and support our prayer. All prayer is Benedictine as all prayer is Christian. There is no right or wrong way to pray, if the time results in compassion and love and drawing near to the Holy One.

Benedictines seek to cultivate and live from a contemplative stance. Theirs is a heart that has and is cultivating a Christ-awareness and Spirit-awareness to perceive and enter into the world as Jesus would. A contemplative stance is a listening and discerning stance, open to the world and ready to learn from the world. This is an embodied listening, ready to change self and not others. A contemplative stance learns to see Christ in all.

Benedictines seek to balance, however imperfectly, silence and solitude with the common life and healthy communication. Work, creative endeavors, and holy leisure also support and build the foundation of Benedictine spirituality. Today most Benedictines are aware that an ascetical practice is a response to the gift of asceticism we receive. In order to cultivate compassion towards ourselves and others, it is necessary to say no to some of the demands made by others seeking our time and talents. Being able to love others because we remove ourselves when appropriate is the way we practice modern asceticism. In an age that craves more and more, interior simplicity reveals a mature heart.

Humility

Benedict's humility is about getting really real, becoming increasingly authentic and dropping pretenses and facades. His teaching on humility comes out of the desert tradition of monasticism where seekers were disengaging from unhealthy aspects of the culture around them in order to have more room in their hearts for God and the heavenly realm. Humility means having a heart open and free to experience God; humility remains a synonym for purity of heart. We never fully arrive; we simply journey in that direction and rely on the grace of God.

Humility allows us to know God more intimately. To the degree that we know ourselves, we also know God; this is not narcissism, but rather the way that God chooses to reveal Self. As we grow in humility, we come to know and understand ourselves as individuals, in community, as members of the human family, and before God. A humble person lives with a huge heart and great capacity to love.

Hospitality

True to the monastic heritage that he received, Benedict exhorted his followers to receive all as Christ. While many are aware of the Benedictine tradition around receiving Christ, Benedict cared how we receive one another. Hospitality leads us back to the common life, whether our common life is shared with a monastic community, a family, a faith community, or a group of friends. Sometimes it is easier to extend hospitality to the stranger who will be in our midst a few days than to the ones who know us best. Our hearts are cultivated when we extend hospitality to all, honoring the Christ in one another. Hospitality proclaims the Immanence of God present in our midst, a reverence for life, Christ's love and compassion. Hospitality is a powerful proclamation of the good news of Jesus.

Benedict (480–ca. 550) and Scholastica (480–ca. 547)

Put your hope in God. . . . Do not wish to be called holy before you really are; first be holy, and then the term will be truer in your case. (RB 4:41, 62)

Around 480, Benedict and Scholastica were born to parents of lesser Roman nobility in the small provincial town of Nursia[1] located in a mountainous region northeast of Rome in present-day Italy. After receiving a local education, Benedict was sent to Rome around 499 to continue his education in classical studies. He grew disillusioned with the decadence: excessive partying, drunken debauchery, sexual promiscuity, political intrigues, and civil unrest. He yearned for something more real and authentic.

Around 500 Benedict left Rome and traveled east toward his beloved Apennine Mountains, settling in the town of Enfide. His emerging reputation for holiness and the reporting of his first miracles distressed Benedict. To escape his growing fame, he moved the following year near Subiaco on the Anio River. Meeting the monk Romanus, he was shown the location of a cave outside of town that would provide the solitude and quiet for which Benedict yearned. He spent the next three years alone, consuming and praying Sacred Scripture, with Romanus serving as his only contact with the outside world.

Benedict hungered for God. His journey into the solitude of the desert, in his case the mountains east of Rome, was a search for an intimate and meaningful relationship with the Holy One. Solitude provided protection from all the distractions that kept him from his singular pursuit of the Divine. As Benedict matured in the spiritual journey, God called him out of solitude to accept disciples in the monastic way of life. He was reluctant to accept followers as mentoring was hard work, and too often mixed motives for entering into the monastic way of life created difficulties.

The next decades were challenging for Benedict. After accepting an invitation to be abbot of a nearby monastery resulted in disaster, he established thirteen monasteries in the region of Subiaco. For twenty-five years, he was tireless in shaping and forming the monks in the monastic way and grounding them in gospel values. When dissension was brewing again, Benedict made the painful decision to leave for the region of Monte Cassino.

The early kernels of his Rule began to take form as he strove to shape and encourage his followers. Many of the men who arrived and sought to join one of his monasteries were newly converted Christians and barely catechized. The new members were from differing social classes, and thus he had to contend with resistance to becoming one with Christ: the unlearned were taught to read, the upper-class learned to do manual labor, and tolerance for diverse cultures was enforced. *Pax* was to be lived out day to day in the manner of treating fellow monks and all guests *as Christ*.

Benedict organized the daily routine of his monasteries to best cultivate and support a life of listening: listening to God, Scripture, other sacred texts, and to one another. Each day was framed with community prayer in the oratory, then periods of time for *lectio* (private prayer and prayerful reading) and manual labor were designated. His desire and intent was to create a lifestyle that taught and encouraged his monks to move deep within and listen to the God who was present.

Around 529, Benedict established one of his last monasteries on Monte Cassino, south of Rome and near the coast, which had once been a temple to Apollo. Here he put the finishing touches on his Rule, intended only for his monks. He did not intend for a religious order to result.

Little is known of his sister, Scholastica. She may or may not have been a nun or a solitary, but clearly she was a woman of strong faith and most likely educated. The stories from St. Gregory the Great's *The Life of Saint Benedict*, written in 593–594, reveal a woman in intimate relationship with God as well as deeply devoted to her brother Benedict. She traveled to Monte Cassino in order to visit her brother, who rarely left his mountaintop monastery and more rarely was away overnight. She visited him, not the other way around as one might expect. Further, after Benedict refused to stay the night with her at the guesthouse near his monastery, it was Scholastica who was sufficiently confident of God's love for her that she went straight to God in supplication that her desire for an extended visit might be provided, and it was.

It turned out to be Scholastica's last visit, and three days later she died. Benedict chose to place her remains in the crypt that he had prepared for himself, located in the oratory of St. John the Baptist.[2] Benedict died sometime between 547 and 550 and was placed in the crypt next to his sister. Gregory tells us that "their souls were always one in God."

In 581 the Lombards destroyed the monastery at Monte Cassino and the monks fled to Rome, establishing a monastery near St. John Lateran. Benedict and Scholastica are venerated as saints. Benedict was formally canonized in 1220 and declared Patron Protector of Europe by Pope Paul VI in 1964.

The following excerpts from St. Gregory's biography of St. Benedict reveal hearts responsive to God and toward one another yet fully human.

From *Gregory the Great: The Life of Saint Benedict*

> There was a man whose life was holy. His name was Benedict, and he was blessed by grace and by name. From his earliest years he had the heart of an old man. Precocious in his way of life beyond his age, he did not give himself up to sensual pleasure. He could have had a good time in this life but he disdained to do so—as if he already saw the bloom of the world as a faded thing. He was born into a free-man's family in the district of Nursia and was sent to Rome to study the liberal arts. But he saw that many of the students there had fallen into vice. So, hardly had he entered the world than he recoiled from it, fearing that the worldly knowledge he had just begun to acquire would suck him down entirely into its bottomless whirlpool. He renounced study, put aside his father's residence and fortune and, desiring to please God alone, he went in search of the monastic habit in order to live a holy life. Thus he quitted his studies, learnedly ignorant and wisely unskilled.[3]
>
> ***
>
> His sister Scholastica had from her infancy been dedicated to the Lord almighty. She used to come to see the man of God once a year. He would come down to meet her a short distance outside the gate, on the monastery property. One day she came as usual, and her venerable brother came down to her with some disciples. They devoted the whole day to the praises of God and to holy conversation. As the shades of night were falling, they ate their meal together. They were still eating, and it was getting late as they continued their holy talk, when his sister, the holy nun, put this request to him: "I entreat you, do not leave me tonight so that we may talk on till morning about the joys of the heavenly life." "My sister," he replied,

"what are you saying? It is completely impossible for me to remain outside my cell."

At the time, the sky was so serene that not a cloud was to be seen. When she heard her brother refuse her, the nun placed her hands on the table with fingers intertwined and rested her head on her hands to pray to the Lord almighty. When she raised it up again, such a violent thunder and lightning and such a downpour of rain broke out that neither the venerable Benedict nor the brothers who were with him could put a foot outside the door of the place where they were sitting. For the nun, while laying her head on her hands, had spilt streams of tears on the table, and this was how she changed the serenity of the sky to rain. Nor did the inundation begin a little after her prayer, but the prayer and the downpour were so closely related that she raised her head from the table along with the thunder and it was at one and the same moment that she raised her head and the rain fell.

Then the man of God, amid the lightning, thunder and immense downpour of rain, seeing that he could not return to the monastery, began to complain sadly: "May God almighty pardon you, sister! What have you done?" "See," she replied, "I asked you and you wouldn't listen to me. I asked my Lord and he listened. Go now, if you can. Leave me and go back to the monastery." But he had to stay under the roof. He was not willing to remain freely in the place so he had to stay unwillingly. And so it happened that they passed the whole night in vigil and each fully satisfied the other with holy talk on the spiritual life.

It was of this incident that I said that he wanted something but could not prevail. For if we consider the thought of the holy man, evidently he would have liked the good weather he had while going down to have continued but, contrary to his wishes and by the power of almighty God, he found a miracle coming from a woman's heart. Nor is it any surprise that the woman who wished to see her brother for a longer time was on this occasion stronger than he, for according to the words of John, "God is love," and by an altogether fair judgment, she was able to do more because she loved more.

The next day, the venerable woman returned to her own cell and the man of God to his monastery. And then three days later, as he was in his cell, he raised his eyes to the skies and saw the soul of his sister leaving her body and penetrating the secret places of heaven under the form of a dove. Overjoyed by her glory, he thanked almighty God in hymns of praise, and he announced her death to the brothers.

Further, he sent them at once to bring the body to the monastery and to place it in the tomb which he had prepared for himself. In this way it happened that those two whose minds were always united in God were not separated in body by the grave.[4]

***

As it was already nighttime, the venerable Benedict went to rest in the upper part of his tower and the deacon Servandus in the lower. There was a stair leading from the lower to the upper part. In front of the tower was a larger building where the disciples of both abbots were asleep. Benedict, the man of the Lord, having advanced the time for night prayers, was already at his vigils while the brothers were still asleep. He stood by the window praying to the Lord almighty. All at once, in the middle of the night, he looked up and saw a light spreading from on high and completely repelling the darkness of the night. It shone with such splendor that it surpassed the light of day, even though it was shining in the midst of the darkness.

A marvelous thing followed in this contemplation for, as he himself related afterwards, the whole world was brought before his eyes, gathered up, as it were, under a single ray of sun. The venerable Father, while straining his attentive gaze on this splendor of shining light, saw the soul of Germanus, bishop of Capua, carried up to heaven by angels in a fiery sphere.[5]

***

In that same year when he was to leave this life, he foretold the day of his most holy death to some disciples living with him and to others living some distance away. He told the former to keep silent about what they heard and explained to the latter what kind of sign would be seen when his soul would leave his body.

Six days before his death, he ordered his tomb to be opened. Soon he was attacked by fever and was weakened with severe suffering. As the illness grew worse every day, he asked his disciples to carry him into the oratory. There he strengthened himself for his departure by receiving the Body and Blood of the Lord. While the hands of his disciples held up his weak limbs, he stood with his hands raised to heaven and breathed his last breath amidst words of prayer.

On that same day a revelation concerning him came to two brothers, one of them resting in his cell, the other a long way off, in the form of the self-same vision. For they saw a road going in an easterly direction covered with carpets and shining with innumerable lamps which led from the cell right up to heaven. Above stood the shining figure of a man in venerable array who asked them if they knew whose road it was. They admitted that they did not. So he said to them, "This is the road by which Benedict, beloved of the Lord, ascends to heaven." Thus the death of the holy man was seen by the disciples present and was also made known to those absent by the sign foretold to them.

He was buried in the oratory of blessed John the Baptist which he himself had built after he had destroyed the altar of Apollo.[6]

The Venerable Bede, Monk of Jarrow (ca. 673–735)

The twelfth step of humility is achieved when a monk's humility is not only in his heart, but is apparent in his very body to those who see him. . . . Due to this love, he can now begin to accomplish effortlessly, as if spontaneously, everything that he previously did out of fear. He will do this no longer out of fear of hell but out of love for Christ, good habit itself and a delight in virtue. Once his worker has been cleansed of vices and sins, the Lord will graciously make all this shine forth in him by the power of the Holy Spirit. (RB 7:62, 68-70)

I, Bede, servant of Christ and priest of the monastery of St. Peter and St. Paul which is at Wearmouth and Jarrow . . . was born in the territory of this monastery. When I was seven years of age I was, by the care of my kinsmen, put into the charge of the reverend Abbot Benedict and then of Ceolfrid, to be educated. From then on I have spent all my life in this monastery, applying myself entirely to the study of the Scriptures; and, amid the observance of the discipline of the Rule and the daily task of singing in the church, it has always been my delight to learn or to teach or to write.[1]

In the northern most reaches of Britain near Hadrian's Wall a monastery was established at Wearmouth in 674. Benedict Biscop, a Northumbrian nobleman, dedicated his first foundation to the Apostle Peter. Within a few years, probably around 679, a gifted child, Bede, entered and began his education.

A second foundation was established at Jarrow in 682 dedicated to the Apostle Paul. St. Ceolfrid was appointed its first abbot. Young Bede was sent to be part of this new foundation. The plague hit the region in 686. The young Bede and his abbot were among the few who struggled to chant the full Divine Office when the other monks were ill or dead.

Wearmouth-Jarrow became a great cultural and intellectual center. Each monastery contained superb libraries, in large measure due to the extensive travels of Abbot Benedict Biscop who brought home manuscripts from all over continental Europe. He also brought back glass, relics and paintings (useful in a mostly illiterate society). On his return from his fifth visit from Rome, Biscop brought back John, the archcantor for St. Peter's, to teach the monks the Roman liturgy and uncial script.

While clearly monastic, Wearmouth-Jarrow was not Benedictine in the strict sense of the word. Benedict's Rule would not become the norm for several more centuries. Rather Biscop, following the common custom of his day, devised a rule based on Benedict's Rule and the rules of the seventeen monasteries that he had visited.

Bede remained at his monastery in Jarrow for most of his life; he did not travel further than Lindisfarne to the north and York to the south. Instead he was a dedicated teacher and scholar as well as an acute observer of life in Anglo Saxon England. His command of Latin was exceptional; he also held considerable knowledge of Greek and, to a lesser extent, Hebrew. He composed dictionaries, encyclopedias, treatises, biographies, hagiography, and manuals. His most significant contribution was his commentaries on the Old and New Testaments and his *Ecclesiastical History of the English People*, completed about 731.

Bede was thoroughly versed in the writings and Biblical commentaries of major thinkers of earlier times. Due to the high esteem that Bede gave Ambrose, Jerome, Augustine, and Gregory the Great, they became known as the Four Latin Doctors. He had also read Josephus, Eusebius and Isidore. His own commentaries were intended for his monastic community. While it is possible that each began as a homily preached to his community, his homilies were refined in order to be read and savored by his students. His was a mature balance between exegesis and lectio.

Bede's spirituality was clearly monastic, grounded in the Gospels, earlier teaching on the contemplative life, and the monastic tradition that he had received. He lived and taught that each monastic should renounce everything else for the sake of the one necessary thing—God. He taught that the spiritual journey begins when we love our neighbor in caring for them, extending acts of mercy and charity to those in need, visiting the prisoner, and aiding the stranger (see RB 4). The mature Christian goes beyond this to longer periods of contemplative prayer, prayer as a way of life, awareness of our need and hunger for God, and focus on God's presence (love). The monastery was the closest thing to heaven while we dwell on this earth. His spirituality was a *longing for heaven*. When writing or speaking on the importance of the desert as a significant place of spiritual growth, he taught that intimacy with God rather than spiritual combat was what was important. He preached on the centrality of our call to participate in the divine holiness. His goal and desire was a wisdom that was understood and lived out in human lives.

While much of Bede's writings were intended for fellow monastics, he also cared deeply about the evangelization and religious formation of the laity. He made some translations of Biblical texts into the vernacular. He also wanted to see suitable people chosen as teachers of the faith.

Bede died as he lived. One of his disciples, Cuthbert, described Bede's last hours. While aware that he was dying, he continued steadfast in his teaching of his students, dictating texts.

> When it came to the Tuesday before Ascension Day, his breathing became very much worse . . . but all the same he taught us the whole of that day, and dictated cheerfully, and among other things said several times: "Learn your lesson quickly now; for I know not how long I may be with you, nor whether after a short time my Maker may not take me from you." But it seemed to us that he knew very well when his end should be. So he spent all that night in thanksgiving, without sleep; and when day broke, which was the Wednesday, he gave instructions for the writing, which we had begun, to be finished without delay.[2]

Bede distributed his few possessions among his brother monks while speaking of his immanent death. Then Cuthbert continues quoting Bede:

> "Hold my head in your hands, for it is a great delight to me to sit over against my holy place in which I used to pray, that as I sit here I may call upon my Father." And so upon the floor of his cell, singing, "Glory be to the Father and to the Son and to the Holy Spirit"; and the rest, he breathed his last. And well may we believe without hesitation that, inasmuch as he had labored here always in the praise of God, so his soul was carried by angels to the joys of Heaven which he longed for.[3]

Bede died on the feast of the Ascension, May 26, 735, and was buried at Jarrow. In 1020 his relics were stolen and moved to Durham Cathedral and placed in Cuthbert's tomb. In 1370 his remains were reinterred in the Galilee Chapel in Durham Cathedral. The missionary St. Boniface called him "the candle of the Church, lit by the Holy Spirit." Pope Leo XIII declared him a Doctor of the Church in 1899.

The following is from Venerable Bede's Homily for the Feast of Pentecost.

From *Homily II.17 on the Gospels*

John 14:15-21 *Pentecost*

Since we are celebrating today, dearly beloved brothers, the coming of the Holy Spirit, we ought ourselves to live in accord with the solemnity that we are honoring. Indeed we only worthily celebrate the joys of this festival if, with God's assistance, we render ourselves conformable to those to whom the Holy Spirit deigned to come and in whom he deigned to dwell. We ourselves are only suited to the coming and illumination of the Holy Spirit for this reason, that our hearts are filled with divine love, and our bodies are dedicated to the Lord's commands. Hence Truth says to his disciples at the commencement of this gospel reading, *"If you love me, keep my commandments, and I will ask the Father, and he will give you another Paraclete."* Paraclete means "consoler." The Holy Spirit is correctly called a Paraclete because, by producing a desire for the heavenly life, he raises up and restores the hearts of believers lest they falter amidst the adversities of this age. Hence, as holy Church increased, it was said in the Acts of the Apostles, *And it was being built up, walking in the fear of the Lord, and was filled with the consolation of the Holy Spirit* (Acts 9:31).

[The words], *"If you love me, keep my commandments, and I will ask the Father, and he will give you another Paraclete,"* were brought to fulfillment in the disciples themselves. They were proven truly to have loved him, truly to have obeyed his commandments, on that day when all at once the Holy Spirit appeared to them in [tongues of] fire as they were praying in the upper room, and taught them, [putting] in their mouths a diversity of languages (Acts 2:1-4), and made them strong in heart with the consolation of his love. Earlier, however, they possessed the Paraclete himself, namely our Lord sojourning with them in the flesh. By the sweetness of his miracles and the wealth of his preaching they were wont to be raised up and strengthened, so that they could not be scandalized at the persecution by unbelievers. But since by ascending into heaven after his resurrection he had deserted them bodily, although the presence of his divine majesty was never absent from them, he rightly added concerning this Paraclete, that is, the Holy Spirit: *to abide with you forever*. He abides eternally with the saints, always illuminating them inwardly and invisibly in this life, and introducing them to the everlasting contemplation of the sight of his majesty in the future.

If we too, dearly beloved brothers, love Christ perfectly in such a way that we prove the genuineness of this love by our observance of his commandments, I will ask the Father on our behalf, and the Father will give us another Paraclete. He will ask the Father through his humanity, and will give [us another Paraclete] with the Father through his divinity. We must not suppose that it was only before his passion that he was asking on behalf of the Church, and that now, after his ascension, he is not also asking, since the Apostle says concerning him, *Who is at the right hand of God, who also intercedes for us* (Rom 8:34).

We also have as our Paraclete our Lord Jesus Christ. Although we are unable to see him bodily, we recollect what he did and taught in the body, as written down in the gospels. If we commit ourselves with all care to hearing, reading, conferring with one another, and preserving these [deeds and teachings] in heart and body, it is sure that we will easily overcome the hardships of this age—as if the Lord were sojourning with us forever and consoling us. If we love this Paraclete and keep his commandments, he will ask the Father, and he will give us another Paraclete—that is, he will in his clemency pour forth the grace of his Spirit in our hearts, and it will gladden us in the expectation of our heavenly homeland in the midst of the adversities of our present exile. Then we will be able to say with the prophet, *According to the multitude of my sorrows in my heart*, your paraclesis, that is, *your consolations, O Lord, have gladdened my soul* (Ps 94:19).

Therefore [Jesus] said, *"He will give you another Paraclete, to abide with you forever,"* and added, *"The Spirit of truth, whom the world cannot receive."* He is calling "the world" the inhabitants of this world, who are given over to love of it. In contrast, the saints who are aflame with desire for heavenly things are fittingly called "the heavens," as the psalmist says, *And the heavens will proclaim his justice to a people yet to be born* (Ps 22:31), which is to say, "And the most illustrious teachers will proclaim, with mind, voice, and action, his justice to a people, who, coming recently to the faith, desire to be born in him." Thus, anyone searching for consolation outwardly, in the things of the world, is not capable of being reformed inwardly by the favor of divine consolation; whoever yearns after lowly delight cannot receive the Spirit of truth. The Spirit of truth flees from a heart it discerns is subject to vanity, and restores by the light of his coming only those it beholds carrying out the commandments of Truth out of love. Hence when he had said, *"Whom the world cannot receive,"* he added next, *"because* [the world] *neither sees him nor knows him; but you recognize him, for he will dwell with you and be in you."* Unbelievers too saw our Lord and Savior in the flesh before his passion, but only believers could know that he was the Son of God, that he was the Paraclete sent by God into the world. Unbelievers were incapable of seeing the Holy Spirit with their eyes or recognizing him with their minds, since he did not appear to the disciples clothed with a human nature, but preferred to come to them, to remain among them, in such a way as to consecrate for himself a most welcome abode in their very hearts. This is what [the Lord] says, *"But you recognize him, for he will dwell with you and be in you."* The one who dwells with the elect invisibly in this life surely provides for them the grace of recognizing him invisibly.

"I will not leave you orphans; I will come to you." Our Lord seemed to unbelievers to be leaving his disciples orphans when he died on the cross. But he did not leave orphans those *to whom he presented himself alive after his passion by many proofs during forty days,* and those to whom he granted the anointing of the Holy Spirit from heaven ten days after his assumption—that is, today. On this point no one who has recognized the inseparable nature, power and working of the holy Trinity disputes that Christ himself came to them.

Following up this matter more extensively, he gives notice of how greatly different their case is *from a nation that is not holy: "Yet a little while and the world no longer sees me. You see me; because I live, you will live also."* Since he said this as he was about to go to his passion, it was but a little while until the completion of his passion; from that time on, the damned were never capable of seeing him again. Only the just, who were saddened by his death, were worthy to see the joy of his resurrection. Those who exulted at seeing him dead had no [reason to] be glad at seeing his resurrection, but they were disturbed and sorrowful on hearing of it, as was fitting.

"You see me," he said; *"because I live, you will live also."* He used a verb in the present tense, *"I live,"* and one in the future tense, *"you will live also,"* undoubtedly because he discerned [that his resurrection] was nigh. Therefore he spoke of the hour in which he would rise to eternal life after destroying death as if it were present. He knew that their life was to be deferred into the future, for each one of them had to struggle up to the predetermined time of their deaths before they could enter everlasting life, and to wait until the end of the age for the resurrection of their bodies. Therefore he said, *"Yet a little while and the world no longer sees me. You see me; because I live, you will live also,"* as if meaning, "*Yet a little while* and those who love the world will see me no more as a mortal; they will be unable to see me rising from the dead because they do not know that life whose glory only those who love my resurrection are worthy to

contemplate. You will be capable of seeing me after this occurs, because *I live*, brought back from the dead; and you will be worthy to be comforted by the example of my resurrection, because you yourselves will come to everlasting life and the joys of a blessed resurrection."

"On that day you will know that I am in my Father, and you in me, and I in you." The apostles then knew that Christ was in the Father through his being united with the undivided divinity; they knew that they were in Christ through their reception of his faith and sacraments; they knew that Christ was in them through their love for him and their observances of his commandments. He himself said to them, *"If anyone loves me he will keep my word; and my Father loves him, and we will come to him and make our abode with him"* (John 14:23). The apostles surely knew these things then because they had been imbued with them by Christ, and now the entire Church of Christ knows them, because she has been imbued with them by the writings of the apostles. But the just will undoubtedly begin to recognize them in a far more thorough way on that day when they begin truly to live, that is, on the day of [their] resurrection, when they begin to know more perfectly all the things that are to be known, to the extent that they endlessly look from closer by, at the very font of knowledge. There is no doubt that this happens to some of the more perfect saints even before the time of their resurrection—to those, namely, who because of confidence in their good works are capable of saying with the Apostle, *I long to die and be with Christ* (Phil 1:23); and, *For me, to live is Christ and to die is gain* (Phil 1:21). . . .

Today is the annual celebration of this event; this is the always-welcome festivity of [the bestowal] of heavenly grace. In order to stamp the memory of this more firmly on the hearts of believers, a beautiful custom of holy Church has grown up, so that each year the mysteries of baptism are celebrated on this [day], and as a result a venerable temple is made ready for the coming of the Holy Spirit upon those who believe and are cleansed at the salvation-bearing baptismal font. In this way we celebrate not only the recollection of a former happening, but also a new coming in [the font] of the Holy Spirit upon new children by adoption.

Therefore, you dear ones, be attentive, to how the type and figure of the feast of the law is in agreement with our festivity. When the children of Israel had been freed from slavery in Egypt by the immolation of the paschal lamb, they went out through the desert so that they might come to the promised land, and they reached

Mount Sinai (Exod 12:2–19:1). On the fiftieth day after the Passover, the Lord descended upon the mountain in fire, accompanied by the sound of a trumpet and thunder and lightning, and with a clear voice he laid out for them the ten commandments of the law (Exod 19:16–29:17). As a memorial of the law he had given, he established a sacrifice to himself from the first-fruits of that year, to be celebrated annually on that day, namely, two loaves of bread made from new grain, which were to be brought to the altar (Lev 23:5-17). It is obvious to all who read what the immolation of the paschal lamb and the escape from slavery in Egypt meant, for *Christ, our paschal Lamb has been immolated* (1 Cor 5:7). He is the true Lamb who has taken away the sins of the world (John 1:29), who has redeemed us from the slavery of sin at the price of his blood, and by the example of his resurrection has shown us the hope of life and everlasting liberty. The law was given on the fiftieth day after the slaying of the lamb, when the Lord descended upon the mountain in fire; likewise on the fiftieth day after the resurrection of our Redeemer, which is today, the grace of the Holy Spirit was given to his disciples as they were assembled in the upper room. Appearing visibly and externally as fire, it shed rays of the light of knowledge invisibly on their inmost thoughts and kindled in them the inextinguishable ardor of charity.

The elevation of the upper room in the one case, and the summit of the mountain in the other, indicate the sublimity of the commands and the gifts. Because no one who still clings to base desires can either comply with divine commands or be worthy of the gifts from on high, in the one case, as a sign of greater perfection, all who received the Spirit were gathered in the upper room; in the other case, to indicate the hearts of the feeble hearers, the entire group of the people were standing at the foot of the mountain, and a few of the elders had gone partially up the mountain (Exod 19:17, 22-24). Moses alone ascended to its very top, where the divine majesty shone forth in fire and a dark cloud (Exod 19:20). Only the more perfect know how to grasp and observe the deeper and most secret mysteries of the law; the carnal-minded people, content with the external aspects of the letter, and gathered apart, as it were, and below, stood to hear the words from heaven. But now that the grace of the Holy Spirit has been given more extensively, [for people] to understand more fully and fulfill more perfectly the words of the holy gospel, the hearts of the faithful are raised up higher.

There [on Sinai] the crashing of the thunder and the blasts of the trumpet resounded in the midst of flames of fire and flashes of lightning. Here [in the upper room], along with the vision of tongues of fire there came down from heaven a sound as of a strong wind (Acts 2:2). But although in both bestowals, namely of the law and of grace, a sound was heard outwardly, yet here [in the upper room], by a more extensive miracle, when the sound was heard there was present the power of a heavenly gift, which would teach the hearts of the disciples inwardly without a sound. There [on Sinai], after all the legal decrees had been heard, the entire people answered with one voice, *"We will hear and do all the words which the Lord has spoken"* (Exod 24:3). Here [in the upper room], after the assembly of the Church, which was being born, had received the enlightenment of the Spirit, they spoke of the wonders of God in the languages of all countries. Doubtlessly it was thanks to a certain discernment that the observance of the law was given to only one nation, that of the Jews, while the word of the gospel was to be proclaimed to all nations throughout the world, and that proclamations of the Christian faith were to be spoken in the languages of all peoples, fulfilling the prophecy that says, *From the rising of the sum to its setting, praise the name of the Lord; the Lord is high above all nations* (Ps 113:3-4).

In addition, in veneration of the reception of the law, a new sacrifice was ordered to be offered to the Lord annually on the day of Pentecost, from the time of the reception of this grace; and it never stops being carried out spiritually, also on this our festivity. Indeed the Church offers a new sacrifice on this [day], when on the Saturday that marks the beginning of the holy feast of Pentecost, she consecrates to the Lord through baptism a new people of adoption, in a rite that is truly most appropriate, as I noted above. Thus not only is the memory of an ancient happening renewed for the Christian people, but also a new sending of the Paraclete from the Father upon a new progeny, those who have been reborn is celebrated. The apostles too, as soon as they had received the gift of the Spirit, offered a new sacrifice to the Lord on this [day]. After announcing the good news to those who had come together, they converted many of them to the faith; and when they had been reborn in the font of baptism (Acts 2:41), and sanctified by the grace of the Spirit, they offered them as living first-fruits of the New Testament in communion at the Lord's altar. Two loaves of bread made from the first-fruits of the new harvest were rightly ordered to be offered (Lev 23:17), for the Church gathers those it can consecrate to its Redeemer as a new family from both peoples, the Jews and the gentiles. . . .

At this point we must look more carefully, my brothers, at the fact that the Holy Spirit not only bestows perfect tranquility in the future upon the just, but also very great [tranquility] in the present, when he enkindles their minds with the fire of heavenly charity. For the Apostle says, *Hope does not disappoint us, for God's charity has been poured forth in our hearts by the Holy Spirit, who has been given to us* (Rom 5:5). And this is the true rest of souls—nay, this is [their] only rest in this life: to be filled with divine love, to despise the favorable and adverse things of the world out of hope of retribution from on high, to root out earthly desires completely from oneself, to renounce earthly lusts, to rejoice in insults and persecutions that have been inflicted for the sake of Christ, and to be able to say with the Apostle, *Let us glory in our hope* [of sharing in] *the glory of God, but not only that, let us also glory in our tribulations* (Rom 5:2-3). A person who trusts that he can find rest in the delights and abundance of earthly things is deceiving himself. By the frequent disorders of the world, and at last by its end, such a one is proven convincingly to have laid the foundation of his tranquility upon sand (Matt 7:26; Luke 6:49). But all those who have been breathed upon by the Holy Spirit, and have taken upon themselves the very pleasant yoke of the Lord's love, and following his example, learned to be gentle and humble of heart (Matt 11:29), enjoy even in the present some image of the future tranquility. Separated with their whole mind from the turmoil of worldly men, they rejoice always in remembering their Maker's countenance, and thirst after reaching perfect contemplation of him, saying to themselves with the apostle John, *We know that when he appears we shall be like him, for we shall see him as he is* (1 John 3:2).

If we desire to arrive at the reward of this vision, dearly beloved brothers, we must demonstrate that, continually mindful of this gospel reading, we are not subservient to the allurements of the world. Thus we may be capable of becoming worthy to attain the grace of the Holy Spirit, which the world cannot receive. Let us love Christ, and let us observe, by persevering, his commandments, which we possess by beginning [to observe them]. It will come about as [our] just reward that, by loving him, we will be worthy to be more fully loved by the Father; and he himself may deign to present us with a more abundant gift of his love in the future. For, as a result of our loving him now, he grants to us to believe and hope in him, but then [he will grant us] to see him face to face (1 Cor 13:12), and he will manifest himself to us (John 14:21), that is, with that brilliance which he had with his Father before the world began (John 1 7:5), with whom he lives and reigns in the unity of the Holy Spirit, God throughout all ages. Amen.[4]

Romuald of Ravenna (ca. 950–1027)

Let them prefer absolutely nothing to Christ. (RB 72:11)

In many ways the history of Christianity is the history of reform and renewal movements. Humanity seems ever in need of conversion, renewal, repentance, and reform. Since its earliest days in the desert, monastics have longed to return to the primitive Christian experience, to get back to the original message of Jesus and the first expressions of monasticism in Anthony and Pachomius. Reform, however, is hard work, and rarely do those who are being called to reform appreciate having their faults and sin and laxity pointed out. Approaching the first millennium, corruption had seeped into church and society, and crime was rampant. The purchasing of church offices, called simony, was too common. Sexual immorality was commonplace and the debate over mandatory celibacy was, at times, nearly violent. Benedict of Nursia was familiar with those who wore the attire of a monastic or vowed religious, yet whose lives did not reflect a commitment to Benedictine spirituality or the Rule. This era was also a time of multiple reform movements that would continue into the next century.

Romuald was born into a noble family at Ravenna around 950. Around 970 he witnessed his father killing a relative in a duel over a land ownership dispute. Despite his claims to have lived a dissolute and thoughtless life, he was sensitive enough that he was horror stricken at what his father had done. A common way to repent for "death by duel" was forty days' penance in a monastery; on behalf of his father, Sergius, Romuald went to the monastery of San Apollinare in Classe (located on an island off the coast of Venice). After seeing a vision of St. Apollinaris, he wrestled with a call to monastic life, finally entering.

San Apollinare had recently become part of the reform movement of Cluny. St. Maieul of Cluny was its reformer, following more closely and more strictly the Rule of Benedict, especially in its liturgical observances. Cluny would become known for its extensive liturgical services and celebration of Masses throughout the day and night as well as its extensive artwork as an expression of God's presence in our midst. Within three years, Romuald was yearning for an even more strict observance of the Rule. Thus he returned to the mainland near Venice and placed himself under the direction of the hermit Marinus.

Within a few years, Romuald, Marinus, and a newly converted doge of Venice established an austere hermitage near the monastery of San Miguel-de-Cuxa in Catalonia in present-day Spain. Over the next five years, others yearning for a simple and honest monastic life joined them. Romuald trained them in the simple and austere observance of the Rule—silence, solitude, rugged simplicity of lifestyle, prayer, and extending Christ's love to all.

Romuald returned to Italy to help his father, who had converted but still doubted his salvation. Once that crisis was resolved, Romuald began moving about Italy, remaining in assorted places for two or three years, either establishing new small monastic communities and hermitages or reforming those willing to mend their ways. Reform is difficult and hostility was a common reaction: too often what was asked for was not really what was wanted.

In 1005 Romuald went to Val-di-Castro near Fabriano and lived in solitude for two years. Again he wandered about Italy, preaching reform and seeking solitude, then attempted to go to Hungary. His failing health prevented this, but some of his followers were able to go east to evangelize and establish new monasteries; a few were martyred.

In 1012 Romuald appeared at Vallombrosa in the Diocese of Arezzo. He was given land that would come to be known as Camaldoli. Here he built five cells for hermits and a monastery, Fontebuono. In 1013 this became the motherhouse of his reform movement: the Camaldolese Order. He continued his life of solitude at Monte Sitria and Bifolco. Five years later he returned to Val-di-Castro where he died alone in his cell. In 1032 an altar was built over his tomb. In 1466 his body was found to be incorrupt and was moved to Fabriano in 1481.

Romuald, despite the courage and fortitude required of a reformer, was remembered as a humble person with a sense of humor. While many of his behaviors seemed eccentric, he attracted many followers. As with many charismatic personalities, many came to listen to his message of reform and few were able to meet his standard, yet when they left they continued to hold him in high esteem. His gift of tears, a particularly important notion for his followers, were connected to the need to speak to God. Tears of compunction and joy in the silence of a monastic's cell were the invocation of God and the witness to God's presence.[1]

Romuald left no writings, but his impact on church history is significant. He is remembered for the many hermitages and small monasteries that he either established or reformed during his lifetime. He restored the eremitic monastic way of life: small monastic communities (cenobites) with hermitages (eremites) nearby. Wanting to guarantee the autonomy of the eremitical way of life through its own discipline (solitude, silence, prayer without ceasing, fasting), Romuald arranged for these small communities and hermits to live together, but unlike traditional Benedictine communities, their obedience was to the hermit superior. Solitude fostered and nurtured the desire to speak to God and to challenge evil in interior spiritual combat. The goal was love. Eremitic monasticism nurtured the call to preaching, evangelization, and reform work.

One of Romuald's followers, Peter Damian, was a prolific writer and major figure in the reform movement that began in Romuald's lifetime and would last into the next century. Peter Damian wrote the *Life of St. Romuald* in 1042, seven years after his own entrance into Fonte Avellane, founded by one of Romuald's disciples. The intent is clear: Peter Damian presents the holy and revered Romuald as an exemplar of monastic observance and courageous reformer of those who bore the name but whose lifestyle betrayed something else.

From *The Mystery of Romuald*

The Little Rule of Master Romuald

> Sit in your cell as in Paradise. Put the whole world behind you and forget it. Watch your thoughts like a good fisherman watching for fish.
>
> The path you must follow is in the Psalms—never leave it.
>
> If you have just come to the monastery, and in spite of your good will you cannot accomplish what you want, then take every opportunity you can to sing the Psalms in your heart and to understand them with your mind. And if your mind wanders as you read, do not give up; hurry back and apply your mind to the words once more.
>
> Realize above all that you are in God's presence, and stand there with the attitude of one who stands before the emperor.

Empty yourself completely and sit waiting, content with the grace of God, like the chick who tastes nothing and eats nothing but what his mother brings him.[2]

From *The Life of St. Romuald of Ravenna*

(3.) It was not long before Romuald noticed that some of the monks were living rather slackly and that he was not going to be able to keep to the strict path of perfection that he had mapped out for himself. So he began to wonder what he should do and to torment himself with questions and anxieties. From time to time he would take it upon himself to sternly rebuke the way of life of his associates; often to support his case, and to their embarrassment, he would invoke the precepts of their rule. It got to the point where since he persisted in showing up their vices, they began to think of murdering him, considering him a prig, for they had no respect for the words of their junior—and a novice at that—and they were not prepared to put up with his criticisms since they had no intention of changing their way of life.

(4.) [A murder plot having failed] Romuald's desire for perfection grew stronger day by day and he could find no peace. At this point he heard about a certain holy man, by the name of Marin, who was living near Venice as a hermit. The permission of his abbot and brethren being readily granted he set off by ship to visit this holy man and he decided to put himself under his direction. Now Marin, among his other virtues, was a man of great simplicity and integrity. No one had taught him how to be a hermit, he had been driven to the way of life under the impulse of his own worthy desires. . . . Every single day he sang the whole Psalter. But given his ignorance and complete lack of education in the ordering of the solitary life—as Romuald afterward related with some mirth—he would often leave his cell with his disciple and wander up and down the hermitage singing psalms everywhere, twenty under that tree, now thirty or forty under another . . .

(5.) At about this time, Peter—Orseolo by surname—was governor of the Duchy of Dalmatia. He had come to attain this high office [of doge] chiefly because he had given protection to the assassins of his predecessor, Vitalis Candiano . . . These assassins had hatched various plots against Vitalis but all had been abortive until finally they decided to set fire to Peter's house, it being right next door to the doge's palace. In this way they reckoned they would be able to capture the doge and to reduce to ashes all his household.

Peter, who shared the conspirators' confidences, gave his consent to this plan but at a price: it was agreed that in exchange for the burning down of his house the conspirators would entrust Venice to his governance . . . This is how Peter became ruler of Dalmatia but it must be said that once his ambition had been gratified then by the grace of God he suffered pangs of remorse.

Now it so happened there was [*sic*] certain venerable abbot, Guarin by name, who came from the furthest parts of Gaul, whose pious custom it was to make pilgrimages to various places. He chanced to visit the doge who asked him what he ought to do to avoid the danger attendant upon the great crime he had committed. Guarin in turn sent for Marin and Romuald; all three agreed that Peter should give up both the world and the office of doge which he had unlawfully assumed and that since he had unjustly acquired for himself the lofty role of despot he ought now to submit to the authority of another. Peter felt that someone in his position could not risk publicly undertaking a conversion of this kind but that the following plan was feasible: it was about to be the feast day of a certain holy martyr whose church was in his possession; on the day before the feast he would send his wife ahead of him, giving the impression that he would shortly follow. . . . In fact once his wife had left he and a great friend, John Granedigo by name, an accomplice of the original plot, together with the three holy men already mentioned, would board ship, and set sail for Guarin's monastery in Gaul. This is how it came about that Peter and John became monks in the monastery of Saint-Michel-de-Cruxa while Romuald and Marin went on to a place not far from the monastery to resume the solitary life to which they were accustomed. A year had barely passed when Peter and John joined them in order to undergo with them the rigors of solitude.[3]

(24.) While the venerable man was at Tivoli he performed another good deed which I do not think should be passed over in silence. There was a certain holy man by the name of Venerius who had from the start lived in a monastery with such humility and simplicity that all the brethren despised him and made fun of him claiming that he was quite crazy. Some used to box his ears, others to tip over him the dirty water in which they had washed their hands and feet, others to injure him by hurling insults. It seemed to him that with so many terrible things going on he could find no peace, so leaving this company behind him he hurried off to live in solitude. For six years he followed a very strict ascetic regime drinking no wine and eating no cooked food. On being asked what rule he was following and to whom he owed obedience he replied that he was his own master and that he followed his own judgment as to what was profitable. To this Romuald replied: "If you carry the Cross of Christ it is essential that you do not forsake Christ's obedience. Go therefore and once you have obtained the permission of your abbot you may return and live here under his jurisdiction in a spirit of humility. And so the edifice of good works your noble intentions is building will become taller through humility and be beautified by the virtue of obedience." By offering this advice and much more besides Romuald taught Venerius how to contend against mental temptations and how to repel the threats of evil spirits. He then cheerfully took his leave of a man now strengthened and enlightened in many ways.[4]

(31.) Romuald spent three years near Parenzo. During the first year he built a monastery; for the next two he lived as a recluse. It was there that his God-given piety brought him to the summit of perfection so that under the inspiration of the Holy Spirit he was able to see into the future and to penetrate with the rays of his intelligence many of the hidden mysteries of the Old and New Testament. For some time he had wanted the gift of tears but however hard he tried he could not experience the compunction of a contrite heart. One day, when he was singing the Psalter in his cell he fell upon the following verse: *I will instruct you and teach you the way you should go; I will counsel you with my eye upon you* [Ps 32:8]. Immediately an abundance of tears welled up in his eyes and he received such illumination in the understanding of divine Scripture that on that very day, and thereafter for the rest of his life and whenever he wanted, he could easily burst into tears and many mysteries of Scripture were no longer hidden to him.

(35.) [After frustrating experiences in the Tuscan Apennines at the monastery of Biforco] Romuald . . . began an eager search for some place where his work would be more fruitful. He sent messengers to the counts of the province of Camerino. At the very mention of his name they were filled with joy and showered him with offers, not only of woods and mountains but also, should he want them, of fields. At last a site just right for the eremitic life was found surrounded on all sides by mountains and woods. In the middle was a large clearing suitable for cultivation and irrigated by an abundant supply of water. This place was formerly known by the name of Val di Castro and had already a small church where a community of holy women were living. These women relinquished the place, new cells were built, and Romuald settled down to live there with his disciples. Who has either the ink or the words to describe how great was the harvest of souls the Lord acquired there through his work? Men flocked to him to seek penance, to give alms to the poor, others left the world altogether and fervently hastened to adopt the monastic life. The most blessed Romuald was like a seraphim afire in the most remarkable way with divine love and wherever he went he set others alight with the fire of his preaching. . . . Among others whom he reprimanded he took to task especially those secular clerks who had gained ordination by paying money and unless they chose to resign he held them to be heretics and utterly damned. Because this was a revolutionary notion the clerks who got to hear of it endeavored to kill him. For throughout the whole region up to Romuald's time the custom of simony was so widespread that hardly anyone knew this heresy to be a sin. To those who argued with him Romuald said, "Bring me your books of canon law and from your own texts you can confirm whether the things I say are true or not." When they had carefully perused these they acknowledged the accusation and lamented the error of their ways. The holy man accordingly established certain rules and taught the clerks who had been living in a secular fashion to obey their superiors and to live together in communities. A number of bishops who had entered into their holy offices through the heresy of simony came flocking to him to do penance. They placed themselves in his hands, promising to relinquish their sees at a fixed date and claiming that they would not delay in taking up the monastic life. And yet out of all these I do not know whether the holy man, as long as he lived, was able to convert a single one. The poison of this heresy was so deep-rooted and so entrenched especially in the episcopal order that such heretics were always full of promises but always put off their execution from day to day, endlessly deferring any decision to the future.[5]

(52.) In Sitria the venerable man spent nearly seven years as a recluse and for all that time observed a vow of silence. And yet even though his tongue was silent his life spoke, so tellingly indeed that scarcely ever before had he worked so hard at converting and bringing to repentance those who flocked to him. Although he was now advanced in years he lived with great asceticism despite the fact that holy men are known to have lived more comfortably in their old age and to have eased the former rigor of their way of life.[6]

(64.) It was not just the likeness of name that made Sitria seem like Nitria; it was also the life there. Everyone went about barefooted, neglecting their bodily needs, everyone was pale and lived with the utmost austerity. Some indeed behind the closed doors of their cells seemed so dead to the world that they might have been already lying in their graves. No one drank any wine not even if he was suffering from a severe illness. But why speak of the monks when even their servants, those who guarded their sheep observed rules of silence and disciplined each other and underwent penance for idle chatter? O golden age of Romuald, an age which even though it did not know the torments of persecution yet did not lack the spirit of voluntary martyrdom! A golden age, I say, nourishing among the wild beasts of the mountains and woods so many citizens of the heavenly Jerusalem!

(69.) The holy man lived in many other places, he suffered much, especially at the hands of his own disciples. Many miracles were worked through him which nonetheless we are going to omit since we wish to avoid being long-winded. After having lived in so many places and seeing that his end was near he returned to the monastery which he had built in Val di Castro and there he waited for his approaching death. He asked for a cell to be built for him with an oratory in which he could be enclosed so that he could observe his vow of silence until his death. Twenty years before he died he had clearly foretold his disciples that it was to this monastery that he would retire and would there breathe his last; no one was to be present at his death or make anything of his burial. Now it was his intention to be enclosed as soon as his reclusory was made; already by then his body was becoming more and more debilitated by various troubles. . . . For about six months he expectorated heavily from a damaged lung and a severe cough caused problems for his breathing. Despite this the holy man neither took to his bed nor, as far as was possible, did he accept any relaxation of his fast. The day came when his strength was utterly sapped and he was overcome by the assaults of his illness. The sun was already setting when he gave orders to the two brethren with him to leave and to close the door of the cell behind them. They were to return after dawn when they had sung lauds. Unwillingly the two left but they were anxious lest Romuald was about to die and instead of going straight off to rest they hid near his cell so they could keep watch over this cache of precious treasure. After some time they began to strain their ears to catch any noise. They could hear neither bodily movement nor the sound of any voice. Rightly guessing what had happened they rushed forward, pushed open the door, lit the lamp and found him lying on his back, a holy corpse, his blessed soul transported already into heaven. The holy pearl lay there, as if of no importance, but destined thereafter to be placed in the most honored position in the king's treasury. Assuredly he died as he had foretold and had gone to where he wanted to be. . . . Now he glows wondrously among the living stones of the heavenly Jerusalem, he rejoices with the fervent throng of blessed spirits, he is clad with the whitest garment of immortality, and he is crowned by the king of kings with a diadem that will shine forever.[7]

Anselm of Canterbury (1033–1109)

So too there is a good zeal that separates one from evil and leads to God and eternal life. (RB 72:2)

Anselm was born in the ancient city of Aosta, at the foot of the Italian Alps, in 1033. From his earliest memories as a child, he was drawn close to God whom he experienced as loving, immanently present, and approachable. Leaving home after the death of his mother, he went north in pursuit of his studies in the newly emerging universities. He eventually landed at the Benedictine monastery of Notre Dame in Bec in Normandy whose school was led by the brilliant scholar and teacher Lanfranc. He entered the monastery in 1059.

Anselm followed in his mentor's path with a quick and deep and broad intellect that soon led to renown. In 1063, when Lanfranc became abbot of the monastery at Caen, Anselm became headmaster and prior at Bec. A popular teacher, Anselm was recognized as the most brilliant intellect since Augustine of Hippo.

In 1078 Anselm was elected abbot of Bec. He had already begun writing: letters, early prayers, and meditations, as well as his *Monologion*, a dialogue with himself, and his *Proslogion*, written in the form of a prayer to God. Rather than following the traditional pattern for theology of meditating on patristic and scriptural texts, he was using human reason to explore and understand what he believed, thus his famous definition of theology as "faith seeking understanding."

Benedictine scholar Hugh Feiss points out that Anselm's *Prayers and Meditations* are suffused with the essence of the psalms, particularly those that express the longing of the human heart for the vision and peace of God. His words to God were from his heart, revealing a passionate love for God. He wrote of repentance, self-knowledge, mercy, and gratitude.

He combined this keen intellect with a loving heart in a single-hearted pursuit of God. His prayers and meditations express a shift from stately and detached prayer forms of the first millennia to more emotional prayer forms.[2] More than a collection of prayers and meditations, this volume was meant to engage readers' hearts and minds with instruction that was heartfelt and not legalistic. Anselm stated that "the purpose of the prayers and meditations that follow is to stir up the mind of the reader to the love or fear of God or to self-examination. They are not to be read through in a turmoil, but quietly, not skimmed or hurried through, but taken a little at a time, with deep and thoughtful meditation. The reader should not trouble about reading the whole of any of them, but only as much as, by God's help, he finds useful in stirring up his spirit to pray."[3] This serves as a very effective description of *lectio divina*.

Most of Anselm's writings were developed at the urging of his fellow monks, who enjoyed his talks and the resulting dialogue into which he would draw them. One of his early works, *De Grammatico*, was concerned with words and sentences, definitions and analyses. His goal was to encourage students to use language precisely and develop strong critical thinking skills.

In 1092 an itinerant scholar whose teachings were contrary to established church belief publicly claimed that Anselm and Lanfranc supported his unorthodox teachings. Anselm's reply came in the form of a letter to Pope Urban II, entitled *Epistle on the Incarnation of the Word*. The natural teacher used a potentially explosive situation to educate his followers.

While in England on abbey business during this same year, Anselm was forcibly detained by King William Rufus, who insisted he become the new archbishop of Canterbury. Lanfranc had been dead four years with no new archbishop installed. The king, near death and fearing what awaited him after life due to his continuous theft from the church, appeased his conscience by forcibly investing Anselm as archbishop. Despite Anselm's protestations, he found himself the new archbishop. What made his new situation palatable was the monastic community of Christchurch, Canterbury.

Anselm remained devoted to the Benedictine monastic way of life and cultivated rich and heartfelt friendships with the monks at Canterbury. The ordinariness of monastic life, centered on the Rule of Benedict, chanting the Divine Office, and *lectio divina*, nourished his continued ministry. While striving to carry out ecclesiastical reform in England, he remained involved in concerns of the Benedictine world. When issues arose around the care and training of children in the monastery, he wrote a letter to another abbot strongly opposing threats and physical punishment of children: "Are they not human? . . . Are they not flesh and blood like you? Would you like to have been treated as you treated them?" Scholars have pointed out how unusual Anselm's position on children was for his time, when children were routinely treated with "insensate brutality" by the monastic authorities who were supposed to care for them.[4]

Anselm was not much of a politician and his straightforward honesty led to strained relationships with the kings of England. He disagreed over matters of the relationship between church and state with King William Rufus, including his insistence that the king return all stolen monies and property. Disputes over separation of church and state continued with King Henry I; as a result, he spent much of fifteen years in exile.

Exile proved fruitful territory for Anselm's continued writings. In 1098 he completed *Cur Deus Homo? (Why Did God Become Man?)*. He also continued refining *Prayers and Meditations*.

Some scholars identify Anselm with the early beginnings of a theological and philosophical movement called Scholasticism. His carefully developed writings for the ontological argument for the existence of God are rational and intellectual. "Reason and faith, he [Anselm] stoutly maintained, had to be compatible, since both came from God. Use reason rightly and understand faith correctly and there is bound to be accord between them."[5] The passionate love that he expressed for God and for humanity reveals a heart pulsing with compassion. Shannon may best summarize Anselm's writings and example in life: "Perhaps the two important truths our age can learn from Anselm are his absolute confidence in the faith he professed and the joy he took in that faith as he reflected on it, wrote about it, and meditated on it. An age of seekers and doubters, like our own, may well be ready to listen to Anselm. He is a wise, warm-hearted, and personable icon of the Joy of Faith."[6]

Anselm died at Canterbury during Holy Week 1109. He was canonized in 1494 and declared a Doctor of the Church in 1720.

From Anselm's *Proslogion, or Discourse on the Existence of God*

Chapter 1. *Exhortation of the mind to the contemplation of God*

> Up now, slight man! flee, for a little while, thy occupations; hide thyself, for a time, from thy disturbing thoughts. Cast aside, now,

thy burdensome cares, and put away thy toilsome business. Yield room for some little time to God; and rest for a little time in him. Enter the inner chamber of thy mind; shut out all thoughts save that of God, and such as can aid thee in seeking him; close thy door and seek him. Speak now, my whole heart! speak now to God, saying, I seek thy face; thy face, Lord, will I seek (Ps 27:8). And come thou now, O Lord my God, teach my heart where and how it may seek thee, where and how it may find thee.

Lord, if thou art not here, where shall I seek thee, being absent? But if thou art everywhere, why do I not see thee present? Truly thou dwellest in unapproachable light. But where is unapproachable light, or how shall I come to it? Or who shall lead me to that light and into it, that I may see thee in it? Again, by what marks, under what form, shall I seek thee? I have never seen thee, O Lord, my God; I do not know thy form. What, O most high Lord, shall this man do, an exile far from thee? What shall thy servant do, anxious in his love of thee, and cast out afar from thy face? He pants to see thee, and thy face is too far from him. He longs to come to thee, and thy dwelling-place is inaccessible. He is eager to find thee, and knows not thy place. He desires to seek thee, and does not know thy face. Lord, thou art my God, and thou art my Lord, and never have I seen thee. It is thou that hast made me, and hast made me anew, and hast bestowed upon me all the blessing I enjoy; and not yet do I know thee. Finally, I was created to see thee, and not yet have I done that for which I was made.

O wretched lot of man, when he hath lost that for which he was made! O hard and terrible fate! Alas, what has he lost, and what has he found? What has departed, and what remains? He has lost the blessedness for which he was made, and has found the misery for which he was not made. That has departed without which nothing is happy, and that remains which, in itself, is only miserable. Man once did eat the bread of angels, for which he hungers now; he eateth now the bread of sorrows, of which he knew not then. Alas! for the mourning of all mankind, for the universal lamentation of the sons of Hades! He choked with satiety, we sigh with hunger. He abounded, we beg. He possessed in happiness, and miserably forsook his possession; we suffer want in unhappiness, and feel a miserable longing, and alas! we remain empty.

Why did he not keep for us, when he could so easily, that whose lack we should feel so heavily? Why did he shut us away from the light, and cover us over with darkness? With what purpose did he rob us of life, and inflict death upon us? Wretches that we are, whence have we been driven out; whither are we driven on? Whence hurled? Whither consigned to ruin? From a native country into exile, from the vision of God into our present blindness, from the joy of immortality into the bitterness and horror of death. Miserable exchange of how great a good, for how great an evil! Heavy loss, heavy grief, heavy all our fate!

But alas! wretched that I am, one of the sons of Eve, far removed from God! What have I undertaken? What have I accomplished? Whither was I striving? How far have I come? To what did I aspire? Amid what thoughts am I sighing? I sought blessings, and lo! confusion. I strove toward God, and I stumbled on myself. I sought calm in privacy, and I found tribulation and grief, in my inmost thoughts. I wished to smile in the joy of my mind, and I am compelled to frown by the sorrow of my heart. Gladness was hoped for, and lo! a source of frequent sighs!

And thou too, O Lord, how long? How long, O Lord, dost thou forget us; how long dost thou turn thy face from us? When wilt thou look upon us, and hear us? When wilt thou enlighten our eyes, and show us thy face? When wilt thou restore thyself to us? Look upon us, Lord; hear us, enlighten us, reveal thyself to us. Restore thyself to us, that it may be well with us, thyself, without whom it is so ill with us. Pity our toilings and strivings toward thee since we can do nothing without thee. Thou dost invite us; do thou help us. I beseech thee, O Lord, that I may not lose hope in sighs, but may breathe anew in hope. Lord, my heart is made bitter by its desolation; sweeten thou it, I beseech thee, with thy consolation. Lord, in hunger I began to seek thee; I beseech thee that I may not cease to hunger for thee. In hunger I have come to thee; let me not go unfed. I have come in poverty to the Rich, in misery to the Compassionate; let me not return empty and despised. And if, before I eat, I sigh, grant, even after sighs, that which I may eat. Lord, I am bowed down and can only look downward; raise me up that I may look upward. My iniquities have gone over my head; they overwhelm me; and, like a heavy load, they weigh me down. Free me from them; unburden me, that the pit of iniquities may not close over me.

Be it mine to look up to thy light, even from afar, even from the depths. Teach me to seek thee, and reveal thyself to me, when I seek thee, for I cannot seek thee, except thou teach me, nor find thee, except thou reveal thyself. Let me seek thee in longing, let me long for thee in seeking; let me find thee in love, and love thee in finding. Lord, I acknowledge and I thank thee that thou hast created me in this thine image, in order that I may be mindful of thee, may conceive of thee, and love thee; but that image has been so consumed and wasted away by vices, and obscured by the smoke of wrongdoing, that it cannot achieve that for which it was made, except thou renew it, and create it anew. I do not endeavor, O Lord, to penetrate thy sublimity, for in no wise do I compare my understanding with that; but I long to understand in some degree thy truth, which my heart believes and loves. For I do not seek to understand that I may believe, but I believe in order to understand. For this also I believe,— that unless I believed, I should not understand.[7]

Chapter 14. *How and why God is seen and yet not seen by those who seek him.*

Hast thou found what thou didst seek, my soul? Thou didst seek God. Thou hast found him to be a being which is the highest of all beings, a being than which nothing better can be conceived; that this being is life itself, light, wisdom, goodness, eternal blessedness and blessed eternity; and that it is everywhere and always.

For, if thou hast not found thy God, how is he this being which thou hast found, and which thou hast conceived him to be, with so certain truth and so true certainty? But, if thou hast found him, why is it that thou dost not feel thou hast found him? Why, O Lord, our God, does not my soul feel thee, if it hath found thee? Or, has it not found him whom it found to be light and truth? For how did it understand this, except by seeing light and truth? Or, could it understand anything at all of thee, except through thy light and thy truth?

Hence, if it has seen light and truth, it has seen thee; if it has not seen thee, it has not seen light and truth. Or, is what it has seen both light and truth; and still it has not yet seen thee, because it has seen thee only in part, but has not seen thee as thou art? Lord my God, my creator and renewer, speak to the desire of my soul, what thou art other than it hath seen, that it may clearly see what it desires. It strains to see thee more; and sees nothing beyond this which it hath seen, except darkness. Nay, it does not see darkness, of which there is none in thee; but it sees that it cannot see farther, because of its own darkness.

Why is this, Lord, why is this? Is the eye of the soul darkened by its infirmity, or dazzled by thy glory? Surely it is both darkened in itself, and dazzled by thee. Doubtless it is both obscured by its own insignificance, and overwhelmed by thy infinity. Truly, it is both contracted by its own narrowness and overcome by thy greatness.

For how great is that light from which shines every truth that gives light to the rational mind? How great is that truth in which is everything that is true, and outside which is only nothingness and the false? How boundless is the truth which sees at one glance whatsoever has been made, and by whom, and through whom, and how it has been made from nothing? What purity, what certainty, what splendor where it is? Assuredly more than a creature can conceive.[8]

Chapter 26. *Is this joy which the Lord promises made full?—The blessed shall rejoice according as they shall love; and they shall love according as they shall know.*

My God and my Lord, my hope and the joy of my heart, speak unto my soul and tell me whether this is the joy of which thou tellest us through thy Son: Ask and ye shall receive, that your joy may be full (John 16:24). For I have found a joy that is full, and more than full. For when heart, and mind, and soul, and all the man, are full of that joy, joy beyond measure will still remain. Hence, not all of that joy shall enter into those who rejoice; but they who rejoice shall wholly enter into that joy.

Show me, O Lord, show thy servant in his heart whether this is the joy into which thy servants shall enter, who shall enter into the joy of their Lord. But that joy, surely, with which thy chosen ones shall rejoice, eye hath not seen nor ear heard, neither has it entered into the heart of man (Isa 64:4; 1 Cor 2:9). Not yet, then, have I told or conceived, O Lord, how greatly those blessed ones of thine shall rejoice. Doubtless they shall rejoice according as they shall love; and they shall love according as they shall know. How far they will know thee, Lord, then! and how much they will love thee! Truly, eye hath not seen, nor ear heard, neither has it entered into the heart of man in this life, how far they shall know thee, and how much they shall love thee in that life.

I pray, O God, to know thee, to love thee, that I may rejoice in thee. And if I cannot attain to full joy in this life may I at least advance from day to day, until that joy shall come to the full. Let the knowledge of thee advance in me here, and there be made full. Let the love of thee increase, and there let it be full, that here my joy may be great in hope, and there full in truth. Lord, through thy Son thou dost command, nay, thou dost counsel us to ask; and thou dost promise that we shall receive, that our joy may be full. I ask, O Lord, as thou dost counsel through our wonderful Counsellor. I will receive what thou dost promise by virtue of thy truth, that my joy may be full. Faithful God, I ask. I will receive, that my joy may be full. Meanwhile, let my mind meditate upon it; let my tongue speak of it. Let my heart love it; let my mouth talk of it. Let my soul hunger for it; let my flesh thirst for it; let my whole being desire it, until I enter into thy joy, O Lord, who art the Three and the One God, blessed for ever and ever. Amen.[9]

Bernard of Clairvaux (1090–1153)

Prefer nothing to the love of Christ. (RB 4:21)

Bernard of Clairvaux was a dedicated reformer, a mystic, a powerful and eloquent preacher, a deep thinker who trusted his own lived experience of God, and a voracious writer, an energetic traveler, statesman, and natural networker who tended to over-commit himself in service to others. His impact on church and society was significant, influencing many thinkers, Catholic and Protestant, during his lifetime and long after his death. He remains controversial to this day.

Born in 1090 in Fontaines-lès-Dijon in Burgundy in present-day France, Bernard was educated by the canons of St. Vorles at Châtillon-sur-Seine, just a few years before the establishment of a new monastery at Cîteaux. This new monastery was the beginning of a monastic reform movement that would be known as "Cistercian." Cistercians follow the Rule of Benedict.

After persuading nearly thirty friends and family to join with him, Bernard entered the new monastery at Cîteaux in 1113 under abbot St. Stephen Harding. In 1115, he was appointed abbot of Cîteaux's new foundation at Clairvaux. In his early years as abbot, Bernard tended to be harsh with himself and his monks and demanded an austere monastic observance. With experience he became more lenient and gracious with his monks while remaining austere himself—to the point of compromising his health. His motivation was the spiritual formation of the monks and reform of monasticism.

Bernard was a prolific writer who made significant contributions in the areas of spirituality, Scripture, and doctrine. Sometime before 1125, Bernard completed writing the treatise *On the Steps of Humility and Pride*.

Around this same time, while living in solitude in order to recover from exhaustion, he wrote a first draft of a series of homilies on the Annunciation that would become *In Praise of the Virgin Mother*. A few years later he wrote *On the Conduct and Duties of Bishops* at the request of an archbishop. This was soon followed by *On Grace and Free Will*. His treatise *On Loving God* was developed between 1126 and 1141. He also wrote a rule for the Knights Templar, called *For the Knights Templar: In Praise of the New Knighthood*. In 1135 he began composing *Sermons on the Song of Songs*.

Bernard's writing also dealt directly with conflicts in the church. Invited to enter the debates between the monks of Cluny (an earlier reform movement of Benedictines) and the Cistercians, he wrote his *Apologia*. Bernard allowed himself to get caught in an eight-year schism when two different men were elected pope: Innocent II and Anacletus II. His contribution led to a resolution. He later found himself mediating a settlement between Roger II, King of Sicily and Pope Innocent II. He continually pressed Rome for the appointment of reform-minded bishops.

Ever the passionate theologian, Bernard publicly challenged theologian Peter Abelard over doctrinal issues. He wrote a treatise called *Against the Errors of Abelard* then launched a major campaign among curial officials to win a public condemnation against Abelard. At the Council of Sens in 1140, he won that condemnation. Unfortunately, other theologians, religious leaders, and bishops received Bernard's public condemnation as well.

As with the harsh expectations he had for his early community, Bernard of Clairvaux may have erred on the side of being too extreme. However, his intentions were honorable: the reform of the church and all its members as well as preservation of the riches of the church's teachings. He perceived his efforts as purging the church of corruption. He desired an honest and humble clergy whose first love was God. For the clerics he wrote *On Conversion* and for monastics *On Precept and Dispensation*. His secretary, Geoffrey of Auxerre, collected his letters and sermons in *Occasional Sermons, Sentences, and Parables*. While publicly preaching against religious movements that he perceived as dangerous and/or heretical, he also began preaching and organizing the second Crusade at the request of Pope Eugenius II who had been a Cistercian monk.

As the Crusade failed in 1148, Bernard wrote *On Consideration*. After Malachy, archbishop of Armagh, Ireland, died while visiting Clairvaux, Bernard wrote *Life of Saint Malachy, Bishop*. In the ensuing years, he revised or completed new works, which included eighteen *Sermons on Psalm Ninety*, and the five books of *On Consideration*.

Bernard of Clairvaux was first and foremost a Benedictine monk. He studied and prayed Sacred Scripture, shaping his heart and outlook on life. He challenged his followers on the seriousness of sin, the need for God's mercy and forgiveness yet the immanent availability of God's mercy. Sin harms the person, and the first step in healing and transformation is to recognize that sin. His teachings on freedom were about interior freedom: freedom from sin and freedom to serve God. He taught that the spiritual journey is a way of life. Because spiritual growth and maturity are a lifelong process, we must cultivate a balance between action and contemplation. He understood that most of his followers had responsibilities and yearned to serve God by serving one another, yet time must be taken to cultivate an interior relationship with God.

The central theme of Bernard's teachings and writings is God's love for us. He understood that love is not selfish but rather selfless and finds its origins in God's love for us. Love leads to a deep union with God and thus with one another.

Bernard of Clairvaux had a powerful intellect, revealed in his writings and homilies, yet he taught that the way to know God is to love God. Knowledge is of value when it is a result of this intense love relationship with God and leads to a heart of gratitude and selflessness.

By the time of his death in 1153, Clairvaux had founded nearly seventy monasteries from Norway and Sweden to the Mediterranean, and nearly one hundred other monasteries became affiliated with Clairvaux and the Cistercian reform. Much of the growth of the Cistercian reform was attributed to Bernard's desire for the holiness of the church, expressed through his tireless travel and preaching, correspondence, and charismatic personality.

Bernard was canonized a saint by Pope Alexander III in 1174 and declared a Doctor of the Church by Pope Pius VIII in 1830. The following excerpt is from one of Bernard's many homilies on *The Song of Songs*, a favorite book of his from the Old Testament.

From *How the Word Visits the Soul*

The Bride speaks:

> Return, my loved one;
> be like a roe or a young hart
> on the mountains of Bethel.

"Return," says the bride. It is clear that the one whom she is calling back is not present, though he was here a little time ago. This is why she seems to be calling him back while he is yet in the process of moving away. Such an urgent summons to return indicates great love in one and great loveableness in the other.

Who are these followers and tireless pursuers of the art of love? One is pursued and the other driven on by such restless love. It devolves on me, as I remember promising, to interpret this text by applying it to the Word and the soul. I confess, however, that even to begin such a task worthily, I need the help of the Word about whom we speak. For such discussion is suited to one more experienced than I, who is knowledgeable in the holy secrets of love. But I may not set aside my duty or ignore your wishes. I see the danger yet I pay no heed, for you compel me. You force me to walk in great matters and in marvels that are beyond me. Alas! I am afraid I shall hear the words, "Why do you narrate my delights and fill your mouth with my mystery?" Therefore, listen to me as one who hesitates to speak yet cannot remain silent. Perhaps my very hesitation will make amends for my daring as, even more, will any profit that you may gain. And maybe even these tears will be viewed in the same light.

"Return," says the bride. So the bridegroom was going away and now he is called back. Who will unseal for me the mystery of this changing scene? Who will give me an adequate explanation for this going and returning of the Word? Is the bridegroom here acting from caprice? How is it possible that the one who fills all things can be said to come and go? What movement in space is possible for one who is a spirit? Indeed, is any movement possible for God, who is subject to no change?

2

This is surely a case in which the principle holds, "Let one who can, grasp it." For our part, let us walk simply and carefully in the explanation of the sacred and mystic language and follow the lead of the Scriptures, which, in mystery, impart a hidden wisdom by human words. In this way, God gains some entry to our experience through the use of images. These propose to human minds the unknown and unseen realities of God by means of familiar likenesses to visible things, as it were offering us what is precious in vessels made of humble materials.

Following the pattern of this chaste language, let us affirm that the Word of God, who is himself God and the soul's bridegroom, comes to the soul and departs from it according to his will. This comes about, however, in the soul's experience rather than because of a movement on the part of the Word. For example, when the soul experiences grace, she recognizes the presence of the Word; otherwise she complains of his absence and again seeks his presence, saying with the Prophet: "My face has sought you; your face I seek, O Lord." And why not? After the withdrawal of such a pleasing bridegroom, surely the soul has no will to desire or even to think about anything else. It follows that she seeks the absent one and calls him back as he moves away.

It is in this sense that the Word is called back. He is called by the soul's desiring, but only the soul who has already experienced his sweetness can have such a desire. For surely desire is a powerful cry. As Scripture says: "The Lord hears the desire of the poor." When the Word leaves the soul, the enduring desire for him becomes a single, sustained cry of the soul, a single, sustained call of "Return," until he come.

3

Now, give me a soul whom the Word is accustomed to visit often, one whom such familiarity makes daring, such tasting makes hungry, and such delightful dallying renders scornful of other pleasures. Give me such a soul and I will unhesitatingly attribute to it both the name and the cry of the bride. I do not think the present text will seem strange to her. It is certainly such a soul who speaks thus. She has, no doubt, shown herself worthy of the presence of the one she calls, even though not worthy of his permanent presence. If this were not the case, she would have called him rather than called him back again, since the use of the word "Return," indicates that it is a matter of calling him back.

Perhaps the bridegroom withdraws for this reason: that he might be sought with greater eagerness and held even more tightly. On one occasion he pretended to go on further. This was not what he wanted; what he wanted was to hear them say: "Stay with us, for the evening is far advanced." On another occasion when he was walking on the sea and the Apostles were in the boat having difficulty with the rowing, he made as if to go past them, not because he wanted to do so, but to test their faith and to draw prayer from them. Eventually, as the Evangelist tells us, they became upset and cried out, thinking that he was a ghost.

This sort of kindly pretence, adopted by the Word as part of his saving plan when he was in the body, he continues now that he is spirit. The same zealous activity is performed in a spiritual rather than bodily manner in souls devoted to him. When he passes by, he wishes to be held. When he goes away, he wants to be recalled.

For this is no irrevocable Word. He goes and comes as he pleases, visiting in the morning and putting to the test. His departure is part of his plan, but his return is always entirely voluntary. Both actions are done for a reason and that reason he keeps to himself.

4

Now it is clear why there is always this sort of change in the soul. It is caused by the coming and going of the Word. He himself has said: "I am going and I am coming to you." And: "A short time and you will not see me, and a short time and you will see me." A short time and another short time! How long such a short time is! O good Lord, tell me how can any time be short in which we do not see you? With all due respect for this saying of my Lord, this time seems to me long and unduly extended. Yet both viewpoints are correct. The time of his absence is short for our deserts, but long for our desires. Both aspects can be found in the Prophet's saying: "If he delays, wait for him; for he will surely come and not be late." How can he not be late if he delays? It must mean that what is more than sufficient for our merits is not enough for our desires. A loving soul is borne along by her wishes and drawn by her desires. She pays no attention to merits and closes her eyes to majesty. Instead she opens herself to delight, leaving everything to the Savior and trusting in him.

Thus, fearless and without shame, the soul calls the Word back; boldly seeking his delights and with easy freedom calling out to a lover rather than to the Lord, saying: "Return, my loved one." Then she adds: "Be like a roe or a young hart on the mountains of Bethel." More of this later.

5

But now you must bear with my foolishness for a moment. As I promised, I wish to speak of how this happens in my own case. It is for your benefit that I speak about myself even though it is not good to do so. If you derive some profit from my foolishness then I shall feel better about it, if not, then I shall plead guilty to foolishness.

I admit, in all foolishness, that the Word has visited me many times. When he enters I do not usually advert to his coming. I sense that he is present and I remember that he had been absent. Sometimes I have been able to anticipate his entry, but I have never been able directly to experience either his arrival or departure. I confess that I am ignorant of where he comes from when he enters my soul, and where he goes when he departs. I do not know the manner of his entry, nor how he leaves. This is in accordance with the text of Scripture, "Nobody knows whence he comes or where he goes to." This should occasion no surprise since he is the one of whom it is said: "Your footprints shall not be known." He does not come in through the eyes, for he has no color; nor through the ears, since he makes no sound. It is not through the nose that he comes: he does not mingle with the air, but with mind, to the atmosphere he gives being not odor. Nor does he gain entry through the mouth, because he is not food or drink. He cannot be experienced by touch, since he is impalpable. How then does he find entrance? Perhaps he does not enter at all as he does not come from outside and is not to be identified with any external object. On the other hand, he does not come from inside me: he is good and I know there is nothing good within me.

I ascended to what was highest in me and, behold, the Word loomed loftier. Earnestly I explored the depths of my being and he was found to be yet deeper. If I looked outside, I saw him beyond myself. If I gazed within, he was even more inward. It was then that I realized the truth of what I had read: "In him we live and move and have our being." Happy are they in whom dwells the one by whom they live; happy they who live for him and are moved by him!

6

You might ask how it is that I know the Word has arrived, since all his ways are beyond scrutiny. I know because the Word is living and active. As soon as he arrives within he shakes to life my sleepy soul. He moves, softens and wounds my heart, which previously had been hard, stony and unhealthily intact. The Word begins to root up and destroy, to build and to plant. He waters the arid lands and brings light to the gloom; he opens up what was closed and sets fire to what was frigid. The twisted roads he makes straight and the rough ways smooth. All this is done so that my soul may bless the Lord and all that is within me may bless his holy name.

When the bridegroom comes to me, as he does sometimes, he never signals his presence by any indicator: not by voice or vision or the sound of his step. By no such movement do I become aware of him. He does not enter the depths of my being through my senses. It is only by the movement of my heart, as I have already said, that I perceive his presence. It is by the expulsion of my vices and the suppression of carnal desires that I recognize the power of his might. I am lost in wonderment at the depth of his wisdom when he subjects my secret life to scrutiny and correction. It is from some slight improvement in my behavior that I experience his gentle goodness. It is from the reformation and renewal of the spirit of my mind, that is, of my deepest humanity, that I perceive his beauty and attractiveness. From the consideration of all these taken together I am overwhelmed by his abundant goodness.

7

When the Word departs it is as though you were to remove the fire from beneath a boiling pot. Immediately the water becomes lifeless and lukewarm and begins to cool. For me this is the sign of his departure and my soul necessarily feels sad until he comes back. The usual sign of his return is that my heart within me begins to warm.

Because this has been my experience with the Word, what wonder that I use the words of the bride in calling him back after he has gone away. I am moved by the same sort of desire as she, even though mine is imperfect and less intense. As long as I live, my habitual manner of recalling the Word will be that word of recall: "Return." Whenever he slips away, I will not cease to call out, my cry following him as he goes. And with the cry is the burning desire of my heart that he return, that he come back to give me the joy of his saving help, to give me himself.

I say this much to you, children. As long as he is absent, who is the only source of my enjoyment, nothing else can bring me pleasure. I pray that he will not return empty-handed, but that he will come back in his usual way, full of grace and truth, just as he did yesterday and the day before. It seems to me that this is why he shows himself like a roe and a young hart: truth has the eyes of a roe and grace has the joyfulness of the young hart.

8

I stand in need of two things: the truth from which I cannot hide, and grace from which I do not want to hide. The visitation will be incomplete if either factor is deficient. Truth on its own is so severe that it crushes, and the happiness which grace brings will appear to be without substance if it is not complemented by truth. Truth is a bitter thing if it is not sweetened by grace. If it is not restrained by truth, devotion is superficial and prone to excess and often leads to overconfidence. For many there was no profit in receiving grace because they did not receive in like measure the moderating influence of truth. So they became too pleased with themselves and lost respect for the gaze of truth. They had no regard for the maturity of the roe, giving themselves entirely to the carefree happiness of the young hart. The result was that eventually they were deprived of the grace, which they wished to enjoy in isolation. Even at such a late stage, it could be said to them: Go and learn what this means, "Serve the Lord with fear, and trembling pay him your homage." When that holy soul said in the midst of her good fortune, "I shall not be moved," all at once she sensed that the Word had turned away his face. So was she not only moved, but quite upset. Thus she learned that it was her task to cultivate not only the gift of salvation but also the burden of fear.

The fullness of grace is not to be found in grace alone nor in truth alone. What does it profit you to know what should be done if the will to do it is not also given? What use is the will if power is lacking? I know many persons who have been made sadder by the recognition of the truth. They can no longer excuse themselves on the ground of ignorance; they know what the truth teaches, but still do not do it.

Hildegard of Bingen (1098–1179)

God will be glorified in all things. (RB 57:9)

Hildegard of Bingen was an unusually gifted woman involved in many facets of public life in her day. She corresponded with bishops, popes, religious leaders, and kings. She has rightly been called a prophet and artist, musician and composer, visionary and mystic, naturalist, healer, poet, and playwright. She traveled the realm preaching Christ and challenging corrupt clerics to return to their original call. Above all else, she was thoroughly Benedictine.

Hildegard was born to a wealthy family in 1098 in the town of Bermersheim near Alzey in the diocese of Mainz in present-day Germany. A common practice among devout Catholics in the past, she was a tithe child as the tenth child and thus offered to God and the church. At the age of eight, she was given to the anchoress Jutta von Spanheim who then educated and trained her in the monastic way of life. Jutta was an extraordinary woman who continued to attract followers and students. Soon her solitary anchorhold became a budding and growing Benedictine monastery.

After Hildegard received a rudimentary education, the monk Volmar of Disibodenberg was assigned to deepen and broaden her education: Sacred Scripture and especially the psalms, the teachings of the Church Fathers, and the Rule of Benedict. Volmar was also a trusted friend and spiritual director. He was aware of his student's history of extraordinary visions.

In 1114, at the age of sixteen, Hildegard made her monastic profession. With the death of Jutta in 1136, she was elected abbess of her community. She had hidden her visions, which had continued from her youth, from everyone but Jutta and Volmar, in large measure because she was concerned that her visions were not subjective personal revelations, rather they were objective theology intended for the broader church. She did not want to deceive herself or others by incorrect teaching; she struggled for years to find the exact words to articulate the visions she received.

In 1141, Hildegard received a prophetic vision commanding her to write and proclaim what God had entrusted to her. She resisted the call, falling ill and wrestling with the Mystery of God, whom she experienced as the Living Light as well as a dark and zealous God who demanded her deepening trust. Aided by Volmar, who had become her secretary, and the nun Richardis, she began writing *Scivias* or "Know the Ways of God." As she began writing, her illness lifted.

Cistercian Abbot Bernard of Clairvaux affirmed her gift as originating in God, encouraging her to share her visions with the church. In 1147, Pope Eugenius read from Hildegard's writings to the assembled bishops at the synod in Trier and publicly affirmed her visionary gifts. The pope urged her to write her visions down.

In 1150 Hildegard moved her community away from the monks at Disibodenberg and began construction of a new monastery at Rupertsberg near Bingen on the Rhine River. She was effectively declaring her independence from the monks and becoming her own autonomous authority as abbess. During this time, and continuing into the future, she composed many hymns and sequences that would eventually become her *Symphonia Armonie Celestium Revelationum* or "Symphony of the Harmony of Celestial Revelations."

Hildegard continued writing. She composed a natural history, *Physica*, and a medical book, *Causae et Curae*. Between 1158–1163 she composed *Liber Vitae Meritorum* or "The Book of Life's Merits" that depicted thirty-five virtues or powers of God confronting vices. Also during this period she made extensive preaching tours to cathedrals and markets in Mainz, Würzburg, Wertheim, Ebrach, Kitzingen and Bamberg, along the Rhine and Mosel rivers. On Pentecost, 1160, she openly preached in Trier.

In 1163, she began her last great visionary book called *Liber Divinorum Operum*, or "The Book of Divine Works." This work of cosmology would take her ten years to complete. During this time, she continued with her writing and preaching tours.

Hildegard confronted popes for their laxity and emperors for their politicking. When an eighteen-year schism between the pope and Emperor Frederick Barbarossa resulted in the emperor declaring the pope deposed and appointing a series of counter popes, she eventually intervened. She challenged the emperor for acting on his own whims and against the good of the church.

In 1178 an excommunicated nobleman was buried in Hildegard's monastic cemetery, which led to her community being placed under interdict. She believed that this man had been reconciled with God before his death, but church authorities demanded that his body be removed from sacred ground. This interdict prohibited all liturgical services, both the celebration of Mass and the Liturgy of the Hours. While this experience was painful, Hildegard and her community stood their ground, refusing to remove the remains. She managed to get the interdict lifted in 1179, shortly before her death on September 17th of that year.

Hildegard's use of words was unique and exacting, the result of her struggles to articulate her powerful experiences of the Divine and of her grappling with theological complexities. Eventually her sisters painted then embroidered her visions in accordance with her exacting instructions.

Hildegard's writings reveal a woman who allowed all of life to teach her as a revelation of the Divine in her midst. Wisdom personified, which she freely referred to as the feminine *sapientia* or *sophia*, permeated her writing and teaching. She was a systematic and dogmatic thinker who added a creative element to her teachings. She expressed her love and gratitude to God in her poetry and music; she encouraged her sisters to celebrate the gift of life in the performance of her plays. Finding the traditional chant taught her by the monks to be too heavy and in a key too low for most women, she wrote her own style of chant—complicated and yet unique—that was better suited for her sisters. She was a woman of her times; aware of her power as minor nobility, an educated Abbess, and a powerful woman, she used her gifts to the advantage of her sisters and to call the clergy and politicians to reform.

In the first selection, the italicized words are from Hildegard's original vision and the words that follow are her explanation of that section of her vision. The second selection is from her extensive liturgical works that are used in Liturgy of the Hours, the celebration of Mass, and other celebrations.

From *Scivias*

The Creation of Adam

> *Then that same flame extended its glowing heat to a little clod of sticky earth which lay below* means that when all the other creatures had been created, the Word of God, in the strong will of the Father and

in the love of supernal sweetness, looked on the poor, fragile matter of the soft and tender frailty of humanity, from which both good and bad were to come, lying heavy and insensate, not yet aroused by the passionate breath of life; *and warmed it, so that it was made flesh and blood*, that is, infused it with the freshness of warmth, since earth is the bodily material of humanity, nourishing it with moisture, just as a mother nurses her children; and *breathed on it so that a living person was raised up*: since He aroused him by heavenly virtue and marvelously drew forth a man discerning in body and soul.

When that was done that bright fire offered the person, by means of the same flame which burnt ardently with a steady incandescence, a shining white flower, suspended in that flame as a dewdrop hangs on a blade of grass, since, when Adam was created, the Father, who is the most bright serenity, gave Adam, by means of His Word, the sweet command of shining obedience in the Holy Spirit, adhering to the same Word in the fresh greenness of fruitfulness; this is because the most sweet liquor of holiness drips from the Father to the Holy Spirit by means of that same Word, producing abundant fruits, just as the pure moisture descending on the grass makes it ready to sprout. *The person sniffed its perfume briefly, but did not savor it in his mouth or touch it with his hands*, meaning he approached the command of the law with his intelligence, as if sniffing it, but did not receive its full force by tasting it, nor by the work of his hands did he fulfill it with complete blessedness. So *turning himself away, he fell into thickest darkness, from which he could not raise himself*—since he turned his back on the divine precept, at the counsel of the Devil he fell into the gaping jaws of death, because he sought God neither in faith nor in works; whence weighed down by his sins he could not rise to true knowledge of God until He came, who was entirely obedient to His Father and entirely without sin.[1]

From *Symphony of the Harmony of Celestial Revelations*

"Sequence for the Holy Spirit"

O fire of the Spirit, the Comforter
life of the life of all creation.

Holy are you, giving life to the Forms.
Holy are you, anointing
the dangerously broken;
Holy are you, cleansing
the fetid wounds.

O breath of sanctity,
O fire of charity,
O sweet savor in the breast
and balm flooding hearts
with the fragrance of virtues.

O limpid fountain,
in which it is seen
how God gathers the strays
and seeks out the lost:

O breastplate of life
and hope of the bodily frame,
O sword-belt of honor: save the blessed!

Guard those imprisoned
by the foe,
free those in fetters
whom divine force wishes to save.

O mighty course
that penetrated all,
in the heights, upon the earth,
and in all abysses:
you bind and gather all people together.

From you clouds overflow, winds take wing,
stones store up moisture,
waters well forth in streams—
and earth swells with living green.

You are ever teaching the learned,
made joyful by the breath
of Wisdom.

Praise then be yours!
You are the song of praise,
the delight of life,
a hope and a potent honor,
granting rewards of light.[2]

"Song to the Creator"

O Word of the Father,
you are the light of the primal dawn

in the rim of a wheel,
accomplishing all things in divine power.
O foreknowledge of God,
you foresaw all your works
as you willed,
so in the midst of your power it lay hidden
that you foreknew them all,
and you acted
as if in the likeness of a wheel
encompassing all,
a sphere that had no beginning
nor is it cast down in the end.[3]

"Antiphon for Divine Wisdom"

Sophia!
you of the whirling wings,
circling encompassing
energy of God:

you quicken the world in your clasp.

One wing soars in heaven
one wing sweeps the earth
and the third flies all around us.

Praise to Sophia!
Let all the earth praise her![4]

"Hymn to the Virgin"

Hail, high-born,
glorious, inviolate Maid!
You are the pupil of chastity,
the matrix of sanctity, pleasing to God.

For this supernal flood
was within you,
as the supernal Word
put on flesh in you.

You are the shining lily
on which God gazed
before all creation.

O fairest and sweetest one,
how greatly God delighted in you
when he set within you
the embrace of his warmth,
so that his Son
took milk from you.

For your womb held joy
when all the harmony of heaven resounded from you;
for as a virgin, you bore God's own Son
when your chastity shone bright in God.

Your flesh held joy
like the grass when the dew falls
and floods it with living green.
So it was in you also,
O Mother of all joy.

Now let the whole Church flush with gladness
and resound in harmony
for the sake of the Virgin, sweetest
Mary, deserving all praise,
the Mother of God.
Amen.[5]

Gertrud the Great of Helfta (1256–1302)

> *But as we progress in the monastic life and in faith, our hearts will swell with the unspeakable sweetness of love, enabling us to race along the way of God's commandments.* (RB, Prologue 49)

Gertrud was born on the Feast of the Epiphany, January 6, 1256. Nothing is known of her family; she vaguely referred to herself as an orphan. At the age of four, she entered the new Benedictine monastery of Helfta, whose abbess was Gertrude of Hackeborn, and began her education at the monastery's school.

Gertrud was bright, affectionate, and astute. She excelled at her studies, which probably included grammar, rhetoric, dialectic, music, geometry, arithmetic, astronomy, literature, and philosophy. As a novice, instruction would also have included liturgy, Scripture, the Rule of Benedict, patristics, and writers in the monastic tradition. She continued in her intellectual pursuits, doing her own scriptural exegesis, and learning to write a fluent German and Latin.

Gertrud thrived in a monastery that was renowned for its culture, learning, and liturgical practices. Daily chanting of the psalms, reading of Scripture texts at the Divine Office, and time given each day to *lectio* filled her heart and mind with the language and imagery of the Bible. She wrote some spiritual works along with some simplifications and explanations of the Bible. Most likely she joined her other sisters in copying manuscripts and teaching in the monastery school.

During Advent of 1280, Gertrud experienced a powerful conversion experience, sliding deep into a spiritual desert that left her depressed and spiritually empty. One month later, she emerged far more spiritually aware and mature, having received a vision of Christ that challenged her mediocrity and laxness in prayer and monastic observance. This dramatic shift left her hungering for God and she began to place far less emphasis on intellectual pursuits that she had devoted herself to before. She transformed from a seeker of the intellectual to a seeker of God who yearned to behold the face of the Divine.

Around 1289, Gertrude began writing a short spiritual autobiography known today as *The Herald of God's Loving-Kindness*. She prayerfully meditated and pondered on her profound conversion experience, working on this autobiography over a nine-year period. Of the five parts to *The Herald*, only the twenty-four chapters of Book Two are her autobiography and written in her own hand. Book One is her vita; Books Three, Four, and Five contain remembrances of Gertrud, notes taken by her fellow nuns, and pieces probably dictated by Gertrud over the years.

Soon thereafter she began writing her *Spiritual Exercises*, a compilation of prayers, hymns, meditations, and reflections on a life of prayer. The first four exercises are loosely organized around themes and liturgical rites: one on re-birth in baptism and three on monastic profession (clothing, consecration, and profession). Exercises five, six, and seven are more specifically liturgical in nature: discipleship, union with God, praise of God, and preparation for death.

Gertrud's spirituality was deeply liturgical and monastic. She commingled the liturgical with the scriptural and the mystical. Her mysticism is significantly Christ-centered. She was devoted to the full humanity of Jesus as one with the Spirit and fully part of the Trinity. She experienced an intense love for the Eucharist. Her use of bridal imagery was common for her era: her use came from the Song of Songs as well as the writings of Bernard of Clairvaux.

Gertrud held a deeply positive attitude toward life. She believed that despite our sinfulness, God is our completion. Life's meaning is found in death, the gift of being with God. Baptism, communion, and confirmation are sources of rebirth and renewal. A key theme in her writings is the spiritual journey, or pilgrimage, whose destiny is heaven and union with God. Faith serves as the walking staff and the goal of the journey is interior freedom and union with God.

Gertrud, along with Mechtild of Hackeborn, is known for her devotion to the Sacred Heart of Jesus. While this devotion is not original to Gertrud and Mechtild, they gave it a framework and structure and made this devotion explicit. Theirs was a devotion to the actual physical heart of the incarnate Son of God, a heart that is fully human and fully divine. The litany of the Sacred Heart, adapted mostly from the writings of Gertrud and Mechtild, is theologically accurate and formational. The essential point of the devotion to the Sacred Heart is the unity of the

Trinity with humanity. Gertrud taught that the Sacred Heart is our merciful advocate before the God who is all loving-kindness.

Gertrud's writings reveal a nun faithful to *lectio divina*, a practice of slow and meditative reading where the seeker listens with the ear of the heart for subtle echoes in the text that reverberates in the heart. *Lectio* shapes heart and mind. *Lectio* prepared her heart to enter into liturgical celebrations: both Eucharist and Liturgy of the Hours. In her writings, she quotes Scripture at length. Benedictine scholar Maximilian Marneau's analysis[1] of Gertrud's writings reveals an excellent theologian. Although her visions had a significant emotional impact on her, her writing of these visions remained theologically accurate and consistent.

Benedictine scholar Miriam Schmitt noted that Gertrud used creative expressions for her understanding and experience of God:

> Among her favorite expressions for the God-Beyond is the phrase "the ever-peaceful, refulgent, and resplendent Trinity." The Father is frequently addressed as the "abyss of omnipotent power," the Word as "inscrutable wisdom," or "abyss of uncreated wisdom," and the Spirit as "amazing charity," "ocean of charity," or "uncreated love." Gertrud emphasizes the nearness of God in Jesus Christ by using light, fire, and creation-centered imagery such as "eternal solstice," "continual fountain of inestimable pleasures," "eternal springtime," "Paradise of unchanging delights," and "imperial morning star, fulgent with divine brightness."[2]

Gertrud was a much-sought spiritual director, both by her community and those outside the monastery. Portions of her writings were copied and shared among her fellow nuns and laity. Apparently, soon after her death, circulation of her writings slowed; her writings did not endure for centuries, as did those of Mechtild of Hackeborn and Mechtild of Magdeburg.

Gertrud was never canonized, although the universal church honors her Feast on November 16. Pope Benedict XIV gave her the title "the Great" in honor of her spiritual depth and theological insight.

In the following excerpts Gertrud attempts to describe her conversion experience and her understanding of the Holy Spirit's activity in her inner life.

From *The Herald of God's Loving-Kindness*

How the Lord first Visited Her as the Dayspring from on High

> May the deep of uncreated wisdom call to the deep of wonderful Omnipotence, to praise and exalt such breath-taking Goodness,

which guided the overflowing abundance of your mercy down from on high to the valley of my wretchedness! (Ps 41:8).

I was twenty-five years old. It was the Monday (a Monday most beneficial for me) before the Feast of the Purification of Mary, the Lord's most chaste mother, which fell on 27 January that year, (ad 1281) at the longed-for time after Compline, as dusk began. You, O God, Truth shining brighter than every light yet more inward than every hidden secret, (Augustine, *Confessions* 9:1) had resolved to temper the thick mist of my darkness. You began gently and easily (Gen 50:21) by calming that storm which, for the past month, you had stirred up in my heart. By that tempest, I believe, you were attempting to pull down the tower (Gen 11) of vanity and worldliness into which my pride had grown, even though I bore—an empty boast—the name and habit of the religious life. All this you did to find a way to show me your salvation (Ps 49:23/50:23).

At the hour already mentioned, then, I was standing in the middle of the dormitory. On meeting an elder sister, according to the custom of our Order I bowed my head. As I raised it I saw standing beside me a young man. He was lovely and refined, and looked about sixteen; his appearance was such as my youth would find pleasing. With kindly face and gentle words he said to me, "Your salvation will come quickly; why are you consumed by sadness? Do you have no counsellor, that sorrow has overwhelmed you?"

While he said this, although I knew I was physically in the place mentioned, it seemed to me that I was in choir, in the corner where I used to make my lukewarm devotions, and it was there that I heard the following words: "I shall free you and I shall deliver you; do not fear." At these words I saw a tender, finely-wrought hand holding my right hand as if confirming what had been said with a promise. He added, "You have licked the dust with my enemies, (Ps 71:9/72:9) and you have sucked honey among thorns; return to me at last, and I shall make you drunk with the rushing river of my divine pleasure!" (Ps 35:9).

While he spoke, I looked and saw that between us (to his right and to my left) there was a hedge of such endless length that I could not see where it ended in front or behind me. On its top the hedge seemed to bristle with such a great mass of thorns that I would never be able to cross it to join the young man. While I stood hesitating because of it, both burning with desire and almost fainting, he himself seized me swiftly and effortlessly, lifted me up, and set me beside him. But then I recognised on that hand, from which I had received the promise already mentioned, the glorious gems of those wounds which cancelled the debts (Col 2:14) of all.

I praise, adore, bless and offer thanks (as far as I can) to your wise mercy and merciful wisdom. For you, my Creator and Redeemer, were trying in this way to make my stiff neck submit to your mild yoke, by concocting with the utmost gentleness a drink suitable for my sickness. For from that time forward, calmed by a new joy of the spirit, I began to go forth in the delightful perfume of your balm, so that I too thought easy the yoke and light the burden (Matt 11:30) which a little before I had reckoned unbearable.

Enlightenment of Heart

Hail, my salvation and the light of my soul (Ps 26:1/27:1). May all that is encompassed by the path of heaven, the circle of the earth (Esth 13:10) and the deep abyss give you thanks for the extraordinary grace with which you led my soul to experience and ponder the innermost recesses of my heart. These had been of as little concern to me before, if I may say so, as the soles of my feet! But then I became anxiously aware of the many things in my heart which would be offensive to your most chaste purity, and of all the other things so disordered and chaotic that my heart could offer no resting place to you who wished to dwell there (John 14:23). But no more than all my worthlessness did this drive you away, Jesus my most beloved, or prevent your honoring me frequently with your visible presence on those days when I came to the life-giving food of your body and blood. Though I could see you no more clearly than one sees things at dawn, nonetheless with kindly condescension you induced my soul to exert itself, that it might be united with you more closely.

I planned to work at achieving this on the Feast of the Annunciation, when you betrothed our human nature to yourself in the Virgin's womb. But you who say "Here I am!" (RB Prol 18, after Isa 58:9 and 70:24) before you are summoned, anticipated that day by forestalling me, unworthy as I was, in the blessings of sweetness (Ps 20:4/21:4). On the vigil of that feast, because it was a Sunday, chapter took place after Lauds. I cannot find the words to describe how you, the Dayspring from on high (Luke 1:78), then visited me through the depths of your loving-kindness and sweetness. Giver of gifts (from the Pentecost sequence, "Veni, Sancte Spiritus"), give me this gift: may I henceforward offer on the altar of my heart a sacrifice of joy, that by my supplication I may win for myself and all those whom you have chosen the privilege of enjoying often that sweet union and unifying sweetness, which was quite unknown to me before that hour! For acknowledging the nature of my life before and since, I declare in utter sincerity that it was a grace given freely and undeservedly. From that time forth you endowed me with a clearer light of knowledge of you, in which the sweet love of your loveliness always attracted me more greatly than the harsh punishment I deserved ever castigated me.

I do not remember, however, having ever enjoyed such fulfillment except on the days when you invited me to taste the delights of your royal table. Whether your wise providence ordered this, or my assiduous neglect brought it about, is not clear to me.

The Pleasantness of the Lord's Indwelling

This was how you dealt with me, this was how you aroused my soul on a certain day between Easter and Ascension. I had gone into the courtyard before Prime and was sitting beside the fishpond absorbed by the pleasantness of the place. The crystalline water flowing through, the fresh green trees standing around, the freedom of the birds, especially of the doves, wheeling in flight, all gave me pleasure: but most of all the secret peace of a secluded place of rest. I began to turn over in my mind what I would like to add to this which would make my pleasure in that resting place seem complete. This was my request: that I might have there a lover—affectionate, able and companionable—to relieve my solitude.

I trust, my God, that it was you—you who produce pleasures beyond price—who had anticipated me and guided the beginning of this meditation; and it was you, too, who drew its conclusion to yourself in such a way. You inspired me with the knowledge that if I poured back like water the flowing streams of your graces with constant and proper thanksgiving, I would grow in a zeal for virtue like the trees and would blossom with a fresh flowering of good works. Moreover, if I looked down on the things of heaven, and if my outer self with its bodily senses were held aloof from hustle and bustle, my mind would be completely at your disposal and my heart would offer you a dwelling-place with all that is pleasant and joyful.

Since my mind had been busy all day long with these thoughts, in the evening when I knelt in prayer, about to sleep, there suddenly came into my mind this verse of the gospel: "If anyone loves me, he will keep my words and my Father will love him, and we will come to him and make our home with him" (John 14:23). Meanwhile my heart of clay realized that you had indeed come and were there present. Oh, how I wish—how many thousand times do I wish—that I could pour over my head all the sea that turned into blood (Ps 77:44/78:44), to flood the cistern of my utter worthlessness in which you, the ultimate manifestation of a worth beyond human thought, chose to live! Or, would that my heart might be given me for an hour, drawn out of my body, to be assayed piece by piece by white-hot coals! Its dross melted away (Isa 1:25), it might offer, if not a worthy home, at least one not as unworthy of you.

For this was how you, my God, showed yourself to me from that time, sometimes more soothing, sometimes more severe, according to whether I was amending or neglecting my life. Although, to tell the truth, if the most painstaking amendment which I ever, even for a moment, achieved had lasted all my life, it could not by any means have merited even the single most severe appearance which I ever experienced after numerous faults and, alas, grave sins. For your great sweetness made you often pretend to be more concerned than angry with what I had done. It seems to me that you showed greater strength of patience in bearing so calmly such great faults of mine than when in the time of your mortal life you bore with Judas the betrayer.

For although I wavered mentally and enjoyed certain dangerous pleasures, when I returned to my heart—after hours and even after days, alas, and after weeks, I fear to my great sorrow—I always found you there. The result is that I could never complain that you withdrew from me for even the blink of an eye from the hour mentioned to the present day, now that nine years have passed. The only exception was on one occasion, eleven days before the Feast of Saint John the Baptist: this happened, so it seems to me, as a result of a worldly conversation on a Thursday, and lasted until the Monday, which was the vigil of the feast (In 1281, the year of Gertrud's conversion, June 23 fell on a Monday), in the course of the mass "Fear not, Zacharias." Your gentle humility, and the wonderful goodness of your wonderful divine love, saw me in such a state of abandoned madness that I did not care that I had lost such a treasure. I cannot recall having mourned its loss or having the least wish for its return. I wonder now what madness had taken my mind prisoner, unless it was perhaps your intention to allow me to have personal experience of what Bernard says: "As we flee you pursue us; we turn our backs and you run to meet us face to face; you plead but are scorned. But no embarrassment or scorn can turn you aside or stop you from acting unwearyingly to draw us to that joy which eye has not seen, nor ear heard, and which has not risen into the heart of man." As I was undeserving in the first place, so you deigned to bestow the joy of your saving presence (Ps 50:14/51:14) on me who had done more than simply fail to deserve it, for it is worse to re-lapse than to lapse; and it has continued to this day. For this be praise and thanksgiving to you—that thanksgiving which, going gently forth from uncreated Love and incomprehensible to all created being, flows back to you.

For preserving so great a gift I offer you that most excellent prayer (1 John 17:1-26) which, as your bloody sweat testifies, the pain of strait necessity made strong, the innocence of pure simplicity made devout and the love of white-hot divinity made potent. By the power of that same most perfect prayer, perfect me completely in union with you and draw me to yourself in my heart of hearts. Then whenever it happens that I must devote myself to external works for practical purposes, may I be given to them on loan, as special cases: then when they have been perfectly completed to your praise, may I return at once to you in my heart of hearts, as the general rule, just as the tumultuous rush of water flows back to the depths, when whatever barred the way has been removed.

For the rest, may you often find me concentrating as much on you as you show yourself to be present to me. By this may you lead me to such perfection as ever your justice permitted a soul to achieve, a soul burdened by the weight of flesh and so completely resistant to your mercy. As it breathes its last within your most strait embrace and most potent kiss, may my soul find itself without delay there where you, unbounded and indivisible, live and are glorious in flourishing eternity with the Father and the Holy Spirit, true God throughout unending ages.[3]

Dame Gertrude More (1606–1633)

Listen intently to holy readings. Give yourself frequently to prayer. . . . And never despair of God's mercy. (RB 4:55, 56, 74)

When England's King Henry VIII broke ties with the Holy See, he began his assault against all his citizens who did not renounce their allegiance to Rome. The church's religious communities became an early focus of his rage. By 1540 the king had suppressed the last of the Benedictine monasteries. Locked in a battle with the Holy See over issues of authority and primacy, he desperately needed revenue for political bribes. The monasteries became his source. The king used monastery lands, the buildings (as their stone was quite valuable), and their contents to win and maintain supporters. Benedictine monks and nuns were imprisoned, killed, or driven underground. The celebration of Mass was outlawed; priests were hunted down and imprisoned or killed. Writings deemed to be "too Catholic" were burned. Some Benedictines slipped out of the English realm[1] and established monasteries on the continent. It soon became evident that a means to connect these houses was needed.

The English Congregation, which connected these English speaking monasteries on the continent, was established in 1619. Each house was committed to continuing the ancient English Benedictine tradition and awaiting the time when it would be possible for religious communities to return to England. These monasteries considered themselves missionaries, returning discreetly to England to revive and sustain the Catholic faith during the persecution against Catholics.

The monks had long hoped for the establishment of an English-speaking community of contemplative Benedictine nuns. Their dream came true when the great-great-granddaughter of the martyr St. Thomas More agreed to join in the creation of such a community.

Dame Gertrude More[2] was born March 25, 1606 and named Helen. Intelligent and outgoing, she received an education from her father Cresacre. Helen was encouraged by a family friend and spiritual director to consider traveling to the continent with the intention of starting a contemplative community of Benedictine nuns. Helen had many reservations. First, with religious life in England outlawed, hence underground and secretive, Helen had no idea what religious life for women was like, especially contemplative and cloistered. Second, she had serious reservations about her own call to religious life. An honest and self-aware woman, she did not want to embark on a journey that was not her true calling.

Trusting in the Holy Spirit, seventeen-year-old Helen, two of her More cousins, and four other Englishwomen traveled to the continent in 1623. A partially restored house in the city of Cambrai, France, became their new monastery. It was initially called the Convent of Our Lady of Comfort and later named Our Lady of Consolation. After formation and a novitiate, Helen took the name Gertrude and made monastic profession January 1, 1625.

Dame Gertrude continued to struggle with her vocation. She remained unconvinced that she was suited to religious life. Further, she and her companions had been formed in the new post-Counter-Reformation[3] spirituality that emphasized mental prayer and intellectual exercises. These exercises or strict meditations were designed for religious in the active life. Her attempts at this structured prayer caused her distress. For her these methodical, rational, and intellectual exercises literally interfered with her own experience of God. The nuns sensed that this was inappropriate to their contemplative way of life, which was intensely interior and intimate with the Divine.

Dame Gertrude suffered deeply but could never bring herself to tell anyone about the depth of her anguish. She questioned her vocation; she questioned her suitability for enclosed monastic life; she questioned her worthiness before God. In 1624, Benedictine Augustine Baker (1575–1641) was sent to serve as spiritual companion and offer courses to the nuns. He was perceived as a non-conformist among Benedictine monks but turned out to be just what the nuns needed. Initially many of the nuns, including Dame Gertrude, spent more time contesting his ideas than pondering what he had to share. Dame Gertrude and he sparred often, yet they grew to like each other immensely. After some months, she finally spoke to him of her spiritual anguish, and with this fierce and intimate conversation she began to experience intense spiritual consolation.

Dame Gertrude's prayer became the simple loving attention to God that was beyond image and word. Within her was a deep and powerful instinct for God, a singular focus on God. She learned to rest on her natural and genuine affection for God.

Baker had recognized that each nun needed to be affirmed in trusting her inner sense of God's movement in her life and dropping the structured meditations that had left the women without consolation. Recognizing that these nuns were intelligent and needed a better collection of books, he began arranging for copies of the best of Catholic texts on the contemplative life to be smuggled out of England. The nuns' library grew quite large; the nuns made and preserved copies of their beloved books and sent copies on to other English-speaking Benedictine houses of women.

Dame Gertrude and her community preserved some English mystical writings that otherwise would have been lost. Among these were Walter Hilton's *The Scale of Perfection*, the anonymous works *The Letter of Privy Counsel* and *The Cloud of Unknowing*, and Dame Julian of Norwich's *Showings (Revelations of Divine Love)*. Scholars tell us that "It is a fact that, apart from a few extracts in one late medieval manuscript, all surviving witnesses to the longer and fuller text of her *Revelations of Divine Love* derive from seventeenth-century English Benedictine sources."[4]

When Augustine Baker's detractors demanded that the nuns of Cambrai surrender all of his writings to be burned, the nuns refused. Instead the nuns compiled all his writings and published them under the title, *Sancta Sophia*. These preserved books found their way into many English monasteries, the British Museum, and several major French libraries.

In 1629, when the monastery needed to choose its first Abbess, both Dame Gertrude and Dame Catharine Gascoigne's names were sent to Rome for consideration. While Dame Catharine was chosen, Dame Gertrude was recognized as the wisdom figure of the community.

Dame Gertrude More died from a virulent form of smallpox on August 17, 1633 at twenty-seven years of age. The monastery in Cambrai continued to grow. In 1793, in the midst of the violence of the French Revolution, the nuns were driven from their monastery at Cambrai, imprisoned at Compiegne for eighteen months, then allowed to return to England in secular dress. These nuns then established Stanbrook Abbey in England.

Dame Gertrude More's jottings and writings were collected by her community and Augustine Baker used them to write her biography, *The*

Life and Death of Dame Gertrude More. This excerpt presents Dame Gertrude's differentiation between the "Simplicitie" of contemplative prayer and the "Complexitie" of mental prayer and intellectual spiritual exercises made popular by the Jesuits. In her informal writings, she argued and exhorted her fellow Benedictine sisters, and all persons of faith, to trust the interior movements of the Holy Spirit to lead them into a mature contemplative life. She was reacting against those of her age who taught seekers to distrust interior movements in favor of their exterior steps or exercises. All her writings were a product of her private ruminations of sacred texts—*lectio divina*.

From *The Life and Death of Dame Gertrude More*

Aptness and seeking after Simplicitie[5]

> The foresaid nobler Propension [Aptness], whereof I have heeretofore spoken so much, and which urgeth the Soule to seeke after God in the interior, doth consequentlie urge her to two things.
>
> The one is to seeke a Simplicitie in her owne soule, which is by denudation of it from all created images, the which Simplicitie onlie makes her capable of an Immediate Union with the Divin Simplicitie.
>
> Secondlie it urgeth her to seeke after the Simplicitie of the pure Divinitie abstracted from all bodies and images of bodies, and from all created images. Hence it is that the soule impelled by the said Propension, that is seated in the Will woulde either not admitte at all of anie discourse, which must consist of Sensible images; or if it do, it takes it but for a meane, and will not allwaies tarie in it, but passes by it unto the Divinitie, that is voide of Image; and this allso without leaving anie image within herself. For this cause the said Propension doth urge the soule not to tarie restingly in the verie noblest image that ever was created, being the Image of the Humanitie of our Blessed Saviour. For either the Soule by the said propension could never make anie use at all of such an image of the Humanitie of our Saviour for tendance to the Divin Simplicitie (which was the case of our Virgin, who could never make use of anie images, nor with profit admitte them into her Soule) or ells if she could make use of them, yet was it but for a time of necessitie for the foresaid ende of attaining to Simplicitie.
>
> And thus you see the reason why soules having the foresaid propension in them, either do not gust or do not allwaies tarrie in Meditation of the Humanitie of our Saviour, nor in praieng to Saints, nor in actuall remembrance and praieng for the dead, or other such

like particuler exercises, the which cannott be donne but by the use of corporall images.

And therefore a soule that is once comme to be able to exercise herself spirituallie (which is by an Exercise of Simplicitie) if she have occasion to beginne her devotions with anie of the foresaid particuler exercises, which must have images in them, she tarries not long in them, but speedilie surmounts them, and enters into the Simple Divinitie, and this in vertue of the foresaid propension, the which ever urgeth the soule (in whome it is) to seeke after the said Divin Simplicitie as it wherein her finall repose and happines consisteth, and which though in our Blessed Saviour it was and is united to a bodie, yet is the Divinitie a distinct thing; and it is the Divinitie, that the soule aspires to for union with it, and to which the said propension doth ever urge her: Our Saviour doth intimate so much in those wordes of his: Si ego non abiero Paracletus non veniet ad vos.[6]

That same *Ego* was [h]is corporall Humanitie or the Image thereof, and the Paraclete was the Simple Divinitie, the which cannott be perfectlie had and enjoied till the corporall image, in which it is, be removed. Like covets the like (saieth the Philosopher) and so doth the soule of man being a spirit (in which the foresaid propension is) thirst after the noblest, yea the perfection of his kinde, being the divin spirit, the which being infinite, the Spirit of the man, that is finite, maie exspatiate, glutte and fill itself in it and with it, and so can it not in anie other things, because they are limited and finite, so that the soule cannott have her satietie in them (besids that things of another kinde are no proportionable foode or pasture for a spirit).

And thus the Divinitie is the infinite and bottomlesse Center and resting place for a mans soule, to whome all other things are but narrow and improper, as be all sensible things. The same Divinitie allso is the proper vast Element, wherein the soule of man should finde life and an infinite life. But furth out of the said Element of hers she is like unto a great whale that were comme into a narrow brooke, that runneth into the sea, in which brooke the whale hath no sufficient scope to swimme and fullie to plunge itself. And therefore it would ever aspire to the Ocean that is for depth and widenes capable of it and of millions more of such, in which Ocean they fine no bottome, and where they exspatiate and swimme in fullnes and securitie from all perills (for they plunge themselves in as deepe as they will, and thereby be secure from perills of other creatures, to which they are onlie subject being out of their said proper dwelling place) and there they enjoie their Element (being water) to their fill and full satisfaction, and are as it were in their kingdome reigning there.

And thus doth a Contemplative spirit in vertue of the foresaid propension, which it allwaies hath in it, ever aspire to his proper Center and Element being the Simple Divinitie, and loves not to make dwelling in creatures, nor in their images, as being neither her proper Center or Element, nor of the spatiousnes and infinitenes which the soule thirsteth after, as wherein onlie she maie have her fill and be secure from all perills whatsoever. For nothing can touch to harme a soule whilst she is immersed in the Divinitie.

And a man maie observe this that I have said even fullie in our Virgins writings both verse and prose, as how that when her buisnes or action is (as most usuallie it is) with the Immediate Divinitie, she there sheweth herself to be in her Element or proper place wherein she freelie, boldlie, spatiouslie and fullie walketh, acteth, swimmeth, and as it were glutteth herself, so that a man maie even see her then to be in her proper element. Some of her verses do intimate somuch unto us as from herself, whereof I shall heere recite ye some:

O I desire no tongue nor penne
but to extoll his praise;
In which excesse I'le melt awaie
ten Thousand waies

If we would die unto our selves
and all things ells but thee,
It would be naturall to our souls
for to ascende and be,

United to our Center deare
to which our soules would hie,
Being as proper then to us,
as fire to upward fly.

O lette us therefore love my God;
for love(s) pertaines to him,
And lett our soules seeke nothing ells
but in this love to swimme;

Till we absorpt by his sweet love
returne from whome we camme
Where we shall melt into that love
Which joieth me to name:

And afterwards she further versifieth thus:

O lette me as the silver streames
into the Ocean glide:
Be melt into that Sea of love
which into thee doth slide.[7]

On Spiritual Exercises and the Contemplative Life

From Multiplicitie and dejection
that would breed our soules confusion,
defende us Lorde with thy Benediction.

Multiplicitie in the foresaid doctrin was indeed but in matter, that in itself was verie good, yea and necessarie for those soules, that are not in tendance to Contemplation, for whome such doctrin is improper and impeditive to the Simplicitie, that they apprehende and seeke after, and is derogatorie or too much restrictive to the Libertie of spirit, that is necessarie for Contemplative Spirits according to the saieng of St Paule, that where is the Spirit of our Lorde (working in a soule) there is (and must be) Libertie and no restreint, whereby the spirit maie worke freelie; and the spirit is not free for working, till it be freed from multiplicitie, and so become simple, and then is it in perfect Libertie, and able to worke towards God in perfection.

And such soules (I meane Contemplatives) do well discerne what tends to simplicitie, and what tends not but is multiplicious. But indeed others that are not in actuall tendance to Simplicitie do not (though they be devout and learned) well discerne the Multiplicitie that is indeed in a doctrin of Multiplicitie, that containeth but good, yea perhaps verie good matter, but do admire such writings and willingly embrace them, and that with good reason. But the other soules do asmuch abhorre them as to their owne practise and that for as good reason in their case, as those former had in theirs.

Our Virgin in her writings (as you have heeretofore heard) speaketh of a riddance, the which indeed is nothing but the freeing of a soule from Multiplicities and other impediments; of which riddance she there saieth that it is so absolutlie necessarie, that without the directer practise that uppon the soule and helpe her by it, in vaine is all the rest he can do to her or for her, as for helping her to attaine to Contemplation.[8] So saied she there. And such riddance by the externall maister is but a concurrence and promoting by him of the foresaid libertie of spirit commended and urged as necessarie by St Paule in the foresaid place, and allso by that other place of his, where he saieth: If you be guided (or carried) by the Spirit, you are not under the Lawe. And indeed in the buisnes of spirituall tendance towards God no doctin or helpe is so necessarie, as that of Riddance towards the procuring of the foresaid Simplicitie, nor anie doctrin or practise more perillous in the buisnes, then counselling to the soule matters, that indeed are of Multiplicitie, or devising, or other imposing on her anie thing more then allreadie by nature or otherwaies lies on her.

And when the soule is come to the foresaid Simplicitie in herself, and freed from all multiplicitie, then is she in the proper and immediat disposition for union with the divin Simplicitie, which is the consummation of all our exercises, and the happines of our soule in it, that is to saie, the happines of this life is had by such union as maie be had in this life, and the happines of the future is in the union, that is proper for that life, being the perfect consummate and supreme happines of the soule. Towards the said happines in this life (according to the degree whereof will be the happiness of the future, and degrees of union there are both heere and there) do and ought all Contemplative Soules to tende (howsoever they reach or attaine, or attaine not thereunto) by the meanes of the foresaid Simplicitie in them, which themselves and their directors are to procure by all possible and lawfull meanes, abhorring (as enimie thereunto) all multiplicities and the occasions thereof.[9]

Blessed Columba Marmion (1858–1923)

The Abbot ought not to teach, arrange or command anything not in accordance with the law of the Lord. Let his orders and teaching be kneaded into the minds of his disciples like the leaven of divine justice . . . he should demonstrate everything that is good and holy by his deeds more than by his words. He should teach gifted disciples the Lord's commands by words, but he will have to personally model the divine precepts for those who are recalcitrant or naïve. (RB 2:4, 5, 12)

Joseph Marmion was born in 1858 in Dublin, Ireland. With his keen mind and intellect, he was fortunate to enjoy access to an excellent education. After completing secondary studies at Belvedere College, he entered Holy Cross College, Clonliffe, and then continued his studies at Catholic University, Dublin.

Marmion first visited Monte Cassino Abbey in 1880 and was deeply attracted to the monastic life. However, he felt obliged to remain with his commitment to diocesan priesthood and was ordained June 1881 in Rome. On his way home to Ireland, he visited the newly built Maredsous Abbey near Namur in Belgium.

Upon arriving in Ireland, Marmion served as a curate, chaplain, and later professor of metaphysics and French at Holy Cross College, Clonliffe. During this time his attraction to monastic life remained strong. He discussed this abiding desire with his bishop; both knew that there was no Benedictine monastery in Ireland for him to consider. He was attracted to the community at Maredsous; finally his Bishop gave his blessing for Marmion to transfer. In November 1886 he entered Maredsous as a novice and was given the name Columba. His first years were hard but he was very happy. He was appointed professor of English at the Abbey School and professor of philosophy to junior monks at the abbey.

In 1899 Marmion was sent to the new foundation of Mont-César in Louvain, Belgium, where he remained for the next ten years as prior and professor of theology at Catholic University of Louvain. He was one of the first to use the expression "liturgical movement," whose aims would attract Benedictines around the world. His desire was to see the Mass and the sacraments more accessible to the laity. He encouraged the laity to follow the liturgical year in their prayer and devotion as did vowed religious. He gave retreats and talks and wrote extensive correspondence.

In 1909 Marmion was elected third abbot of Maredsous. He continued with his retreats, both to his own community and to other religious houses. When the First World War erupted, much of Belgium was occupied by German troops. Belgium had declared its neutrality at the outbreak of the war, but Kaiser Wilhelm violated the border anyway. Remaining in Belgium was a risk for Marmion, an Irish citizen, and monks of other nationalities. They could easily be accused of being spies and/or collaborators with the Germans. Therefore, he took some of his younger monks to Edermine, County Wexford in Ireland to wait out the war.

Between 1917 and 1922, Marmion produced three volumes of spiritual writing: *Christ, the Life of the Soul*; *Christ in His Mysteries*; and *Christ, the Ideal of the Monk*. His writings were influential during the Second Vatican Council (1962–1965), especially while drawing up the Constitution on the Sacred Liturgy. At his initiative, Maredsous and other Belgian monasteries separated themselves from the German Beuronese Congregation due to the strong anti-German sentiments in the region and formed the Belgian Benedictine Congregation.

Always in frail health, Marmion began to deteriorate during a flu epidemic that swept his region. He died at Maredsous of bronchial pneumonia January 30, 1923. He is buried in the monastery cemetery.

Much of Marmion's enduring attraction lies in the simplicity of his teaching. His desire was for the laity to draw close to God and cultivate a loving intimacy with God, and this is reflected in his language. Still, his apparent simplicity pierced the truth of divine precept. Any seeker can understand his writings at first read, but a closer examination yields endless possibility and complexity. Much of his writing began as talks, retreats, and letters. A Benedictine monk rooted in the tradition of *lectio divina*, of savoring texts and allowing one's heart to be shaped by those texts, his work is best savored slowly, not read for intellectual fulfillment alone.

Marmion's basic definition of prayer is simply spending time with God. Cultivating this familiarity with God through prayer remains respectful and results in a heart shaped and transformed. For Marmion, a virtuous life does not come from obeying "shoulds" and "oughts." Rather, we begin by loving God, and in time, we will be led to practice and cherish the virtues.

Marmion stressed the divine response of Christ toward a society that denied and disowned Him. He balanced this with emphasis on the full humanity of Jesus and the centrality of the Incarnation. Love as active verb resounds through his writings. Marmion stressed that it was in Jesus' humanity that he was able to give adoration to his Abba. Marmion called Jesus' loving reverence for the Father *piété*. Another theme in his writings is the mutual and eternal love within the Trinity. God as Trinity of Persons is Infinite Love transcending all our preconceptions and analogies. Yet Trinity is personal, not impersonal; Trinity is relational.[1]

Another theme throughout many of Marmion's writings is divine adoption: "we are by adoption what Christ is by nature." We are called to be sisters and brothers of Jesus Christ and our destiny is eternal life. In piercing the veil of Christ's humanity do we reach the depths of Christ's divinity.

Dom Columba Marmion was declared a venerable June 28, 1999 and a blessed September 3, 2000, during the Jubilee Year.

Excerpt from the final chapter of *Christ, the Life of the Soul*, "Co-heirs with Christ."

> It is fitting . . . that in concluding these talks on the life of Christ within us, we should rest our gaze upon that eternal inheritance Our Lord asked His Father to give us. We ought to think about it often, for it is the final goal of all the work of Christ.
>
> "I came"—I came here below—"that they may have life" (Rom 8:30); but that life is not truly life unless it is eternal. All our knowledge and love of the Father and of His Son Jesus ought to lead to an eternity of that life which makes us children of God. "This is *everlasting life*: that they may know you, the only true God, and Him whom you have sent, Jesus Christ" (Jn 17:3). Here below, we can always lose the divine life that Christ gives us through grace; only death "in the Lord"[2] makes that life permanent, assures it within us in a way that is unchangeable. The Church indicates this truth by giving the name "day of birth" to the day on which a saint enters into eternal possession of that life.[3] Here below, the life of Christ within us is only a dawn; it does not attain its noonday—a noonday, though, which has no decline—unless it comes to its fullness in

glory. Baptism is the wellspring from which the divine river spouts forth, but the river's-end "which makes joyful the city of God"[4]—the city of souls—is the ocean of eternity. That is why we would have only an incomplete idea of the life of Christ in our souls if we did not contemplate the river's-end to which, of its nature, the life should flow.

You know how earnestly St. Paul prayed for the faithful of Ephesus that they might understand the mystery of Christ: "I fall on my knees to the Father," he said, that it might be given to them to comprehend the "breadth and length and height and depth" of this mystery (Eph 3:14, 18); but the great apostle is careful also to show them that this mystery has its crowning only in eternity, and that is why he ardently desires that this thought shall occupy the minds of his dear Christians. "I do not cease to remember you in my prayers," he writes to them, "that the God of our Lord Jesus Christ, the Father of glory, may enlighten the eyes of your mind, so that you may know what is the hope to which He has called you, what are the riches of the glory of the inheritance He has reserved for those that are holy."[5]

Let us, therefore, look at what this "hope" is, what are "the riches" St. Paul had so keen a desire to see known. But has not he himself said that we cannot surmise "what things God has prepared for those who love Him"; that "eye has not seen nor ear heard, nor has it entered into the heart of man" (1 Cor 2:9; Isa 64:4) to know what these marvels are? That is true; everything we say about these "riches of the glory of our inheritance" will fall short of the reality. Let us listen, however, to what Revelation tells us on the subject. We can understand it if we have the Spirit of Jesus, for St. Paul says in the same passage: "The Spirit fathoms everything, even the deep things of God . . . and we have received (at baptism) that Spirit who is from God, that we may know the marvels God has given us,"[6] given us through His grace which is the dawn of glory. Let us listen to Revelation, then—but let us listen with faith, not with the senses; for everything it will tell us is super-natural.

Eternal *beatitude* consists in *seeing* God face-to-face, changeless *love* and perfect *joy*.

Speaking of the theological virtues which come in the train of sanctifying grace and which are like springs from which super-natural activity on the part of a child of God flows, St. Paul says that in our present state here below "there abide faith, hope and charity, these three"; but, he adds, "the greatest of these is charity." (1 Cor 13:13) And what is the reason for that? It is because in heaven, which is the completion of our adoption, faith in God gives place to vision of God, hope vanishes in our possession of God, but love remains and unites us to God for ever.

This is what it consists in, the glorification which awaits us and which will be ours: we shall see God, we shall love God, and we shall joy in God; those acts constitute eternal *life*, an assured and full participation in the very life of God; and hence, beatitude of the soul, a beatitude in which the body is to share after the resurrection.[7]

In heaven, we shall *see* God. To see God as He sees Himself is the first element of this participation in the Divine nature which constitutes the *life* of blessedness; it is the first vital[8] act in glory. Here below, says St. Paul, we only know God by faith, in an obscure manner, but then we shall see Him face-to-face. Today, he says, I only know God imperfectly, but then I shall know Him "even as I am known" by Him (1 Cor 13:12). What it is in itself, this "seeing," we cannot know now. But the soul will be given strength by "the light of glory," which is nothing else but grace itself reaching its full resplendence in heaven. We shall see God with all His perfections: or rather, we shall see that all His perfections come down to one infinite perfection which is Divinity; we shall contemplate the inner life of God; we shall enter, as St. John says, into "fellowship" with the Holy and Blessed Trinity, Father, Son and Holy Spirit; (1 Jn 1:3) we shall contemplate the fullness of Being, the fullness of all truth, all holiness, all beauty, all goodness. We shall contemplate, and for ever, the humanity of the Word Incarnate; we shall see Christ Jesus, in whom the Father is infinitely well-pleased; we shall see Him who has willed to become our "elder brother"; we shall contemplate the Divine features, henceforth glorious, of Him who has delivered us from death by the bloodshed of His Passion, who has given us the ability to live this immortal life. It is to Him that we shall sing a hymn of thanksgiving: "You it is who have ransomed us, O Lord, by your blood; who have established us in your kingdom. To you, praise and glory!"[9] We shall see the Virgin Mary, the choirs of angels, all that multitude of the elect which St. John declares "no man could number" and whom he shows surrounding the throne of God.[10]

This, that we see God without veil, without obscurity, without intermediary, is our future inheritance, is the consummation of our Divine adoption. "The adoption of sons of God," says St. Thomas,[11] "comes about through a certain conformity of likeness to Him who is His Son by nature."[12] This is brought about in a twofold fashion:

here below, by grace (*per gratiam viae*, through grace for the journey) which is an imperfect conformity; in heaven, by glory (*per gloriam patriae*, through the glory of our homeland), which will be a perfect conformity, as St. John said: "My dearly beloved, we are now already children of God; but what we shall one day be has not yet been revealed. However, we know that on the day when God appears in His glory, we shall be like Him, for we shall see him just as He is."[13]

Here below, then, our resemblance to God is not complete; but in heaven it will appear in its perfection. Here below, we have to labor, in the obscure light of faith, to make ourselves resemble God, to "destroy the old self," to let the "new self," created in the image of Jesus Christ, come to its maturity.[14] We have to renew ourselves, perfect ourselves, ceaselessly in order to come near to the Divine model. In heaven, our resemblance to God will be one that has been made complete; we shall see that we are truly children of God.

But this "seeing God" will not put us in the position of an immobile statue, which would prevent our doing anything at all. Contemplation of God will not be the annihilation of our activity. For all that the soul will not cease for a moment to contemplate the Divinity, it will keep free play of all its faculties. Look at our Lord Jesus Christ. Here on earth, His holy soul continuously enjoyed the beatific vision; and yet His human activity was not absorbed by this continuing contemplation; it remained intact, it was manifested by His apostolic journeys, His preaching and miracles. The perfection of heaven would not be perfection if it had to annihilate the activity of the elect.

We shall see God. Is that the whole of it? No: seeing God is the first element of eternal life, the primary source of beatitude; but if the intellect is divinely satisfied by Eternal Truth, must not the will be so too, by Infinite Goodness? We shall *love* God.[15] Charity, says St. Paul, "never ends." (1 Cor 13:8) We shall love God, not with a love that is weak, vacillating, so often distracted by created persons and things, exposed to ruin, but instead a powerful love, a pure love, a perfect and eternal love. If, in this vale of tears where, to preserve the life of Christ within us, we have to weep and struggle, if here below love is already so strong in certain souls that it rends out of them cries that move us to our depths: "Who shall separate me from the love of Christ? Neither persecution, nor death, nor any creature will be able to separate me from God" (Rom 8:35–39)—what will this love be when it embraces Infinite Good, never to lose it? Fervor of soul for God—we gaze and are never sated! Held secure by Love—ever we are at peace! And this love that has no end will be expressed in acts of adoration, of delight, of thanksgiving. St. John shows us the saints prostrated before God and making heaven ring with their praise: "Glory and honor and power to you, Lord, forever and ever!"[16] That is an expression of their love.

Finally, we shall *joy* in God. You have read in the Gospel that Our Lord Himself compares the kingdom of heaven to a banquet which God has prepared in order to honor His Son: "He will gird himself, and have them sit at table, and He will come and serve them." (Lk 12:37) What does this signify if not that God will Himself be our joy? "O Lord," cries the psalmist, the elect "shall be inebriated with the plenty of your house; and you shall make them drink of the torrent of your pleasure. For with you is the *fountain of life*" (Ps 35:9-10)—the very source of life. God says to the soul that seeks Him: "It is I—I myself—who will be your great reward."[17] It is as if He were saying: "I have loved you so much that I have not wished to give you a natural bliss, a natural happiness; I have wished to take you into my own house, to adopt you as my child, in order that you might have a share of my beatitude. I wish you to live by my very life; I wish my own beatitude to become your beatitude. I gave you my own Son on earth. Become mortal by His humanity, He was delivered up for you to merit the grace of your being and remaining my child; He has given Himself to you in the Eucharist under the veil of faith. Now it is I myself in glory who give myself to you, so as to make you a sharer of my life; to be your beatitude without end." The Father "will give Himself because His Son gave Himself; He will give Himself immortal to immortals because His Son gave Himself mortal to mortals."[18] Grace here below, glory above; but it is the same God who gives us them: and glory is but the coming into flower of grace. It is the Divine adoption, hidden and imperfect here below, revealed and complete in heaven.

That is why the psalmist so much sighed after this possession of God: "As the hind longs for running waters, so my soul longs for you, O God." (Ps 41:2) "My soul thirsts for God, for the *living* God." (Ps 41:2) "I shall be satisfied when your glory shall appear" (Ps 16:15)—I shall be satisfied only when your glory, a glory full of delights, shall appear to me.

For that matter, Our Lord Himself when speaking of this beatitude tells us that God causes the faithful servant to "enter into the joy" of his Lord.[19] This joy is the joy of God Himself, the joy God possesses in the knowledge of His infinite perfections, the beatitude God feels in the ineffable fellowship of the Three Persons; the infinite repose and contentment in which God dwells. His joy will be our joy: "that they may have my joy made full in themselves"; (Jn 17:13) His beatitude and repose, *our* beatitude and repose; His life, our life; a perfect life, in which all our faculties will be fully contented.

In this will be found "that full participation in unchangeable good," as St. Augustine excellently calls it.[20] To such an extent has God loved us. Oh! if we knew what God has in store for those who love Him!

And because this beatitude and this life are those of God Himself, they will be, for us, eternal. They will have no end, no termination. "Death shall be no more," says St. John, "neither shall there be mourning, nor cries of pain, nor suffering"; "God will wipe away every tear from the eyes of those who enter into His joy."[21] There will be no sin any more, nor death, nor fear of death: nothing will rob us of this joy. It is *for always* that we shall be with the Lord: "we shall be with the Lord for ever." (1 Thess 4:16) Where He is, there shall we be.

Hear in what strong terms Jesus has given us this assurance: "I give my sheep everlasting life, and they shall never perish, and no one shall snatch them out of my hand. My Father, who has given them to me, is greater than all, and no one will be able to snatch them out of my Father's hand. My Father and I are one."[22] What assurance Christ Jesus gives us! We shall be with Him for ever, with nothing thenceforth being able to separate us from Him; and in Him we shall savor an infinite joy that no one can ever take away from us, because it is the very joy of God and His Christ. "You now," said Jesus to His disciples, "have sorrow"—here below—"but I will see you again, and your heart shall rejoice; and your joy no man shall take from you." (Jn 16:22) Like the Samaritan woman,[23] let us say to Him: "O Lord Jesus, Divine Master, Redeemer of our souls, elder Brother, give us this divine water, that we may never thirst; this water that will make us live. Grant us, here below, to stay united to you through grace, so that one day—as you have prayed your Father for us (Jn 17:24-26)—we may see for ever the glory of your humanity, and rejoice in you, for ever, in your kingdom!"[24]

Raïssa Maritain (1883–1960)

It is love that drives these people to progress toward eternal life. (RB 5:10)

On September 29, 1912, St. Paul Abbey in Oosterhut, Holland, celebrated the final oblation of three new oblates: Jacques Maritain, his wife Raïssa, and her sister, Vera Oumanşov. They had already been living a quasi-monastic life in a household with a daily horarium including Mass, the Liturgy of the Hours, meals together, a chapter meeting, and even a rotating leadership system (a weekly "captain" who acted as superior). A story of the struggle of conversion could be told about any one of the three: Jacques, the Parisian intellectual, Vera, "the little sparkle," and Raïssa, the contemplative. This is Raïssa's story.

Raïssa Oumanşov was born into a devout Jewish family in Rostoff-on-the-Don, Russia. Three years after her birth in 1883, her little sister Vera was born. The two girls were very close. They invented a game that they played often. In it the world was a place where "no one cried or was sick, where flowers and fruits grew all the year round, where children played with birds and could fly like them."[1]

The little girls' world was turned upside down in 1893 when renewed threats of a pogrom convinced the family to emigrate to Paris. Raïssa had been called the *oumnista* or good, intelligent child of her class in Russia and within a few months she learned French well enough to rank first in her class once again. Reading and studying brought her joy.

In her early teens Raïssa entered a disquieting phase. She was reading widely both poetry and prose. Her daily life seemed boring and narrow. She began to have questions about God, but she did not want to ask her parents since they no longer followed the religious practices they had been so devoted to in Russia. Raïssa wrote of that time: "I continued to pray in secret to the God who was disappearing from my mind, but whom my heart would not abandon."[2] She distracted herself from her interior struggles by studying piano, by dancing and talking with other Russian refugees, and by various intellectual pursuits. Still, as she wrote: "nothing succeeded in filling the growing emptiness in my heart. Before all else, I had to make sure of the essential thing: the possession of truth about God, about myself, about the world."[3]

At the age of seventeen she began attending classes at the Sorbonne, seeking that which seemed "necessary in order that human life be not a thing absurd and cruel."[4] At the Sorbonne she met Jacques Maritain, a young Parisian from a liberal Protestant family. They discovered that they both believed in the same quest, namely the examination of essential things. They both wanted to know whether life was "an accident, a blessing or a misfortune."[5] They were both especially moved by questions about suffering—even the suffering of animals demanded an explanation. In the beautiful park, the Jardins des Plantes, they decided "for some time longer to have confidence in the unknown . . . in the hope that to our ardent plea, the meaning of life would reveal itself." However, they also decided to commit suicide together if they could not discover a way of life that made sense to them, "new values" to "deliver us from the nightmare of a sinister and useless world."[6]

Before graduation they became engaged. In Raïssa's words: "Our engagement took place in the simplest way, without any proposal. We were alone in my parents' living room. Jacques was sitting on the rug, close to my chair; it suddenly seemed to me that we had always been near each other, and that we would always be so. Without thinking, I put out my hand and stroked his hair; he looked at me and all was clear to us."[9] For his part, Jacques saw Raïssa as "vivacious, merry, empathetic, with a marvelous smile and an extraordinary light in her eyes."[8]

Two years later, after Raïssa survived a life-threatening illness, they were married on November 26, 1904. Still on their spiritual quest, they opened their home to many literary and artistic friends and to other students of the truth. Through one Catholic writer in particular, Leon Bloy, they also met the saints and mystics of the Christian Classics. Raïssa wrote "the city of God was becoming visible on our horizon, its outlines vague as yet, but already dazzling."[9] On June 11, 1906, Raïssa, Jacques and Vera were baptized. Two years later their community of three was formed.

In their community they studied Scripture and the Christian classics. Eventually they chose the Benedictine mystic Gertrud of Helfta as their spiritual guide, with Thomas Aquinas as their philosophical mentor.

Jacques would become a well-respected teacher of Thomistic philosophy at universities in France and in the United States. Raïssa would follow a mystic path, devoting most mornings to prayer and silence. Vera would be the quiet, practical encourager and helper. Their home became a place of welcome for students and other truth seekers, where they sometimes hosted as many as fifty people. Coming to meetings and seminars, people also came to share their personal problems with Raïssa.

Together Raïssa and Jacques wrote books on prayer, liturgy, and poetry. *Prayer and Intelligence* was their fifty-six page introduction to contemplative prayer. Their book drew on the life and writings of Benedict, Gertrud, Hildegard, and other Christian mystics, and promoted the Benedictine practice of *lectio divina*.

At the outbreak of the Second World War they fled to the United States where Jacques continued teaching and writing. There they wrote another Benedictine-influenced book, *Liturgy and Contemplation*. Making use of the journals Jacques had encouraged her to write, Raïssa also published her first memoirs in two books: *We Have Been Friends Together* (1942) and *Adventures in Grace* (1945). In these she reveals her appreciation for the many friends and mentors in her lifelong search for "the essential thing," and she reflects on her prayerful companioning of others along that same path. A more intimate sharing of her life would not be published until after her death.

Raïssa had never regained her full emotional or physical strength after the near death experience in the summer of 1904. But it was Vera who died first, of cancer, in 1959. Seven months later, on November 4, 1960, Raïssa died from the effects of a stroke that she suffered while on vacation in France.

In 1963 Jacques published *Raïssa's Journal*, based on her notebooks, letters, and other jottings from 1906 to 1960. Catholic university students, first of all, then a wider readership, met Raïssa at the deep heart level. This is Raïssa the mystic, steadfast in her commitment to *oraison* or silence in God's presence. This is one whose heart is being transformed by grace into a heart of humility and compassion. Over the years, in pain and joy, Raïssa grew into utter confidence in God, both "unspeakable light" and "reassuring darkness." As she wrote:

> If I seek to know me, I lose myself in thought—
> It is You Alone who know my real name . . .
> May Your pity rescue us through grace . . .
> Purify, illuminate my soul,
> That it may escape the power of nothingness.[10]

The following excerpts from Raïssa's journals are grouped not chronologically but by theme.

From *Raïssa's Journal*

The Heart of a Mystic

Meudon, January 1936—to Jacques:

Go on loving me like this, I need a great deal of love in order to live and I know that *I* have to love "as not loving," in St. Paul's sense, and beyond St. Paul's sense. What a terrible vocation! It is for that God has placed your marvelous love at my side. For with whom would I have been able to live such a vocation, except with you? And to do so, henceforth, in an extraordinary suspension of all knowledge. Yesterday, nevertheless, I was intensely conscious of the love of the Cross of Jesus and of not wanting to separate myself from that Cross, which brings the just and sinners together.

My beloved, I believe, like you, that "it is a sign from God to be more and more severed from human conceptions concerning the reality of God. His thoughts are not like our thoughts . . . " But, Jacques, to live like this is martyrdom, it is no longer to have anywhere to lay one's head . . .

What is wonderful, is that I can take this rest in our heart without in any way hindering God's action in us. God is so much with you. And you are truly my only sweetness in this world.

3 August 1939

. . . But the morning is the best part of my life, the one from which I draw all my energies; I must at all costs preserve the solitude, silence and stillness of it.

All my happiness is to sit at my table, in front of the window looking on to the garden, and beyond to the green water of the Creuse and the forest on the opposite bank.

When everything is at peace around me and I am quiet and alone, silence with God comes and then I find in my heart everything I love on earth and in heaven. And a landscape of living waters, and a light breeze, and savour and rest and enthusiasm.

21 December 1932—To Antoinette Grunelius

. . . A certain very simple prayer by which we take into our heart those for whom we wish to pray; and then we offer this heart, with all its desires and anxieties to God, in order that He may come into it with all his love, give Himself.

By this very meek aspiration, which demands only a little of one's attention and which, in its simplicity, is a total gift of oneself to God—one attracts to oneself Him who wants above all to give Himself, and set everything on fire with His love, and make every obstacle to his bounty melt away in it.

This very simple prayer can be practiced anywhere and at any time. It brings great meekness into the soul, calms all impatience, melts all hardness at the core of this double, yet single, love of God and our neighbour.

10 March 1919

One must do everything well, especially if one has the perilous honour of serving Truth. Above all one must do no disservice to charity. Christianity is not only a force which makes for order—people have been a little too conscious of that particular aspect of it.

It is a dynamic driving force, in virtue of the charity and zeal which animate it.

The very order it establishes, and guarantees, is not for the good of the few; it is for the good of the greatest number, the common good.

Catholics have too often been the servants of what is least worthy of being served—the servants of those who invoke "order" only in their own interest.

Wednesday, 11 October 1950

Jacques, Vera and I went today to see our friends, the Benedictine nuns of Regina Laudis. Touching welcome. The prioress sweeter than ever.

A Sister I know particularly well is none too happy, she cannot get accustomed to this foundresses' life. And besides she is perturbed by the influences of certain thinkers and theologians . . .

This trouble and agitation one gets oneself into because Catholics have not got *everything* that the Orthodox and the Protestants have that is good, beautiful and original—it's a form of concupiscence (even though its object is spiritual) which is not good; the Church, the unique, unique, [*sic*] holy, mystical Church, at once *visible* and *mystical*, is made up of all spiritual goods—wherever they are found.

The One Thing Necessary

13 July 1921

Of the difficulty of perfection in the world, where one is incessantly obliged to be busy with the management of oneself and of things—where one is at the mercy of all the occasions of acting imperfectly. The religious life is such a considerable help to renunciation.

In the world, in the midst of occupations, distractions and temptations of all kinds, what is there that can replace the boons of the religious life? We were talking about it this morning with Jacques.

Might it not be a greater humility and a more abandoned trust in the mercy of God who will take into account our good will, knowing all the various obstacles?

Yes, in spite of all the deficiencies and all the imperfections and all the sins, let us keep afloat by confidence and by the humble and constant recognition of our spiritual mediocrity.

Let us accept trustfully the state of life in which Providence has placed us. For God can sanctify us anywhere! And we, we might remain just as mediocre if we left the world.

Humility

10 December 1915

Humility, annihilation before God, that is only too easily understood! But the humility of a saint before all creatures? I understand it like this: the creature, even when holy, is of itself that which is not, as God said to St. Catherine of Siena. In thinking oneself above some other soul, one thinks oneself something and therefore one lacks the humility due to God, which is to recognise our own nothingness. Whereas if one does not esteem anything in oneself but recognises a grace as coming from the mercy of God one is not lacking in humility, nor in justice, for one attributes nothing to oneself. Thus St. Paul was able to enumerate a great many graces which had been given him. Usually, when one recognises some good in oneself while comparing oneself to one's neighbor, one behaves like the pharisee. We should never look except at God and ourselves and only concern ourselves with our neighbor to render him service. "It is I who am judge," said the Heavenly Father to St. Catherine Siena, "it is not you." And even if we were to discover nothing to find fault with ourselves, we should not on that account be justified, St. Paul says.

13 July 1921

To love. To abandon oneself. Nothing else is necessary to sanctification. No, nothing, not even silence with God if that is rendered impossible by real obstacles, interior or exterior.

The soul can be sanctified without, so to speak, realising it, and find itself at last united to God without having had the leisure to practice what it would have thought most necessary for this.

Avoid sin, humble oneself because of sin, never be discouraged. Love God, love, love. That is the one thing necessary. All the rest can vary *ad infinitum*.

4 October 1924

Before God, the soul is utterly confident. If it is in fault, it knows that He wants to correct it and forgive it! If it asks for divine grace, for charity, for humility, it knows that its heavenly Father will not give it stones instead of bread. Oh, that is the one thing necessary! To live open before God, to implore him unceasingly to purify our heart. To make every effort not to let ourselves pass over anything; to keep our eyes well open to our defects, to our sins, to make a very strict confession of them.

How good it is to live in the sole desire to please God. As regards our neighbor, only one thing is good: the love which is charity.

God, my God, have pity on me, allow me to live in our presence, with an upright soul, wholly lifted towards You; a sincere soul, drinking in your sweet Veracity; a very humble soul, looking only to you for all its good. But a soul that has also great confidence in its Father's goodness, and receives the manifestations of Your Love as simply as a child.

A Heart Being Formed: Love of Neighbor

31 August 1916

Still the same prayer. It seems to me that God is forming my heart to charity, to humility . . . If I do not accept what my neighbour teaches me, God will not teach me either.

Life hidden in God. Not to see in my neighbor anything but the love with which God loves him, and his wretchedness as a creature which is no greater than my own wretchedness and which makes God himself pity us and draws down his mercy on us. All the rest is vanity and pettiness.

1917

Long interruption in these notes on account of the aridity of the prayer, always the same, and the tedium of always noting the same things. Tiredness too and illnesses.

Versailles, 12 March 1917

Long, ardent absorption in God.

13 March 1917

Have pity on your poor little creature.

17 March 1917

Profound absorption in God.

I want my neighbour to have a shelter in my heart as I myself want to find a shelter in the compassionate Heart of Jesus.

Mystical Prayer: Reassuring Darkness

1924

My soul can no longer accept anything from reflections, comparisons, images, symbols, savours, fervours—even though the light of God glimmers in all these things. It can no longer be nourished except by that utterly pure light, even though to the soul it be darkness and therefore surpassing all understanding.

21 March 1924

St. Benedict— I await all from God.

For from me to Him, it seems that all the bridges are cut. But not from Him to me.

I cannot even direct, be it even in a most general and indeterminate way, my thought in silent prayer.

Direction and light from God alone.

Then the soul subtly perceives the absolute divine transcendence.

Infusion of the divine light.

Incomprehensible and unspeakable light, but which is the very one which the soul desires, to which it aspires, for which it thirsts.

Vivifying and insensible light, at the highest point of the spirit.

In this prayer the soul feels a radical distaste for its own impulses, its preferences, its desires, its sensibilities, its comprehensions.

It is entirely open to God and breathes in the incomprehensible light that comes from Him.

It reposes in the unknown will of God and lives on a wholly spiritual love.

All this is reassuring darkness
insensible delight
incomprehensible communion.

The soul reposes more securely in this darkness than it did in the previous illuminations induced by some creature, image, symbol or sentiment.

It seems to it that it subsists on the sole will of God.

Enveloped by God: Transformed by Grace

Undated (Probably 1958)

We breathe in God, down into the deepest
and most silent recess of the soul.
And the breath we breathe out with our lips
Can be a word and song of love.

Like holy acts, words of wisdom and beauty overflow from contemplation:—the Psalms and the whole of the inspired Scripture.

It is the same with contemplation and song as it is with the river and the sea. The end, the trend of the river is to lose itself in the ocean; but if the waters overbrim their bed, it overflows to right and left. The end of the contemplative soul is to lose itself in God—but the over-brimmed heart pours itself out in songs and in acts.

Undated

God envelops us and penetrates us and his being is unknown to us. We know that he exists, and we do not know what his existence is.

When, liberated by death, and transformed by Grace, we appear before God, we shall know his transcendence, but it will be a total, absolute discovery.

"What eye has not seen, what ear has not heard, what has not entered into the heart of man," that is what we shall know.

Nevertheless this transcendence, this infinite omnipotence above us, far from making us distant from it, is what places us in it without distance.

Our dependence is another absolute which places us in the bosom of God, there where we live on eternal life, there where we are born, through the soul, into eternal life.[11]

Bede Griffiths (1906–1993)

Listen, O my son, to the teachings of your master, and turn to them with the ear of your heart. (RB, Prologue 1)

Bede Griffiths was one of three founders of a Christian Ashram in India and one of the pioneers of the dialogue between Eastern spirituality and Christianity. His roots were thousands of miles from India in an English town called Walton-on-Thames. He was born Alan Richard Griffiths to a middle class family in 1906. He had an older sister and brother. His peaceful and happy childhood was shaken at the age of four, when his father lost his business after being cheated by a partner. Griffiths' father never completely recovered either financially or emotionally from this experience, but the family learned to cope with relative poverty. As an adult, Bede Griffiths would come to embrace simplicity of life not so much as a matter of material necessity but of spiritual necessity.

Griffiths' formal education began when he was twelve at Christ's Hospital, a public school for poor boys. He ranked first in his exams and won a scholarship to Oxford where he read English literature and philosophy at Magdalen College. During his third year C. S. Lewis became his tutor. Their shared agnostic rationalism led them to become great friends in their search for truth and faith.

Griffiths grew up with the traditions of the Church of England, but did not have a deep connection to his faith in his youth. His intellectual curiosity led him to read widely and he gradually drew away from the church. His first encounter with the mystical came during his last term at school. While he walked alone in the evening he had a profound awakening to the natural world around him: "It was as if I had begun to see and smell and hear for the first time. The world appeared to me as Wordsworth describes it with 'the glory and the freshness of a dream.'"[1]

This encounter with nature reveals Griffiths' poetic nature. He counted this as one of the decisive experiences of his life.

Griffiths graduated from Oxford with a degree in journalism, and soon after began an adventure with two friends they called an "experiment in common life." He purchased a country cottage in the Cotswolds and lived there for about a year with Hugh Waterman and Martin Skinner. They were determined to strip their lives of anything to do with the industrial revolution. They slept on mattresses stuffed with straw and lived without water, drainage, or lighting. The three purchased some cows and were eventually able to supply their whole village with milk.

During this time he began reading the Bible for literary interest. It became part of the routine of their lives together to read a chapter of the Old and New Testaments each morning before breakfast. Soon he saw in the Bible the same quality that he treasured in poetry: "I had always understood it to be the function of the poet to see beneath the surface of nature and of human life and to reveal its inner meaning."[2] The need to look beyond the material world became one of the fundamental motifs of his thought and life.

Griffiths had inherited the family prejudice against Catholicism. His mother had once told him that the greatest pain for her would be for someone she loved to become Roman Catholic. Griffiths decided to apply for ministry in the Church of England, and he was advised to work in the slums of London to get some practical skill. This experience was devastating to him and led to a personal crisis. His attempts to regain his equilibrium culminated in a profound spiritual encounter. Griffiths felt an overwhelming need to repent and spent a whole night on his knees meditating on Christ in the Garden of Gethsemane. He reflects on this experience in his autobiography: "Up to this time my religion had been to some extent external. It had engaged my mind and imagination, my feelings and my will, but it had never really touched my heart."[3] In the morning he knew what he needed to do.

Griffiths attended a retreat led by an old priest that was being held that morning for a group of ordinands. The experience touched him deeply: "I had been reborn. I was no longer the centre of my life and therefore I could see God in everything."[4] Soon afterwards he visited Prinknash Abbey where on Christmas Eve, 1931, he received his First Communion as a member of the Catholic Church. A year later he was clothed as a Benedictine novice and received the name of Bede. In 1937 he made his solemn monastic profession and three years later, at the age of thirty-four, he was ordained.

The Rule of Benedict requires each monk to take a vow of obedience and to surrender all personal property. This was no hardship for Griffiths. Monastic life was a natural fit, consistent with his thought and frugal temperament. He found the sharing of property to be rooted in the communal spirit of the New Testament. The surrender of one's will was a free act "made for the love of God." Soon after his solemn profession, Bede was made guest master of the monastery. According to St. Benedict, "All guests who arrive should be received as Christ" (RB 53:1) and met with "every mark of love" (RB 53:3). This spirit of warmth was characteristic of Bede's life. He welcomed all people, those from different backgrounds and a range of experiences. His listening heart made everyone who met him feel valued. Griffiths also extended his hospitality to the spirituality of different faith traditions through his writings and lectures.

Circumstances eventually led Bede to serve in the French monastery of Farnborough where he met Benedict Alapott. Benedict was a European-educated Indian priest who hoped to start a community in India. In time Bede was granted permission to go to India with Benedict. Before his trip he wrote to a friend that in India he would "discover the other half of [his] soul." The two priests left for Bombay in 1955. After a series of pilgrimages and a few years in Bangalore, Bede joined Father Francis Acharya in Kurisumala (Mountain of the Cross). During the ten years he spent there, Bede and Francis melded the Christian faith with the tradition of Indian monasticism. They developed a monastic liturgy using the Syriac rite and dressed in the Kavi orange robes of an Indian Sannyasa.[5] He adopted the Sanskrit name, Dhayananda, which means bliss of compassion. During his time in Kurisumala, Bede studied the culture and religions of India, wrote, and traveled to give lectures on the dialogue between the East and the West.

Bede spent the latter part of his life at Shantivanam, a Christian ashram[6] in South India dedicated to the Holy Trinity. He arrived there in 1968 with two other monks. Here he continued to study Indian thought and relate it to Christianity in his writings. Under his leadership, Shantivanam became a center of contemplative life and a model of interreligious dialogue. Bede traveled extensively during his years at Shantivanam. Even after his first stroke in 1990, he lectured in the United States, England, Germany, and Australia. When he returned, he suffered a series of strokes and died in his hut surrounded by those who loved him. In May of 1993 he was laid to rest in a temple nearby.

During his lifetime Bede wrote numerous books and articles. His last book, published posthumously, is entitled *Universal Wisdom*. This title captures the spirit of a man who embraced everyone and everything as an expression of the divine. Central to his thought is the idea of cosmic revelation: God is revealed through poetry, philosophy, science, nature, and world religions. He viewed all of these things as expressions of the "love-energy of God." Griffiths emphasized the centrality of Christ and saw Christianity as the culmination of humanity's evolving sense of the divine. At the same time, he drank deeply from the wisdom of many faith traditions, especially Hinduism, and encouraged others to do so. He saw the more intuitive, holistic approach to life of the Eastern traditions as an important complement to the almost exclusively rational, analytical outlook of the Western world. In his vision, the East and the West balance and enrich each other. Throughout his life, Bede worked with the marriage of opposites. His writings build bridges between science and the imagination; the rational and mythological; the transcendent and the immanent; matter and spirit; the East and the West. He did this without sacrificing the integrity of each pole.

The ideas that Bede expressed in his writings were not simply products of his intellect, they were an integral part of his being and an organic part of his life. During his lifetime, a visitor to Shantivanam would have seen him wrapped in the homespun marigold yellow cloth of an Indian villager, living in a simple thatched hut, prayerfully immersed in the sacred writings of the East or the West. Bede was drawn to the contemplative core of monastic life. Prayer and meditation were woven through his day. He didn't experience a life of detachment from the material world as a form of deprivation, but as a way to savor the beauty of simplicity and experience God more fully: "When you are detached from the world, you see everything coming from the hands of God, always fresh and beautiful. Everything is a symbol of God."[7] He was always looking beyond the immanent to the transcendent. Although his thinking was rich and complex, he strove to transcend reason: ". . . the moment [Reason] turns inward to its Source and knows itself in its Ground by a pure intuition, then it knows the truth of its own being and the being of the world, and then it becomes really free."[8] The experience of God at the center of one's being is the place of the transforming love that Bede exemplified in his writings and his life.

From *A New Vision of Reality*:

> We all have an urge to transcend ourselves. That is why people want to do things like climbing mountains and going to the moon. It is a need to transcend, to get beyond the self. That is also why we fall in love. We want to get out of our self into another. Clearly we

are drawn out of ourselves all the time, but this impulse towards self-transcendence is only fulfilled when we are drawn back to our source, when we give ourselves back totally to the origin from which we come. That is the ultimate meaning of the impulse of love.

In this process of being drawn back in that way to the source, sin is the refusal to respond. Sin is the refusal to love. Love is drawing us back to itself. It has given us our being, put us in this world with all its problems, but it is always drawing us back. This instinct of self-transcendence is the movement of love. Also each person's creation is a movement of love. The Father wills us, loves us into existence. He conceives us in the Word and wills us in the Spirit, and he expresses his love in bringing us forth. We are an effect of that divine love, and the very love which sends us forth from him draws us back to him all the time. If we respond, then we grow in this world and gradually we are transformed, as Jesus was in the resurrection, and we return to the Father. Sin, on the other hand, is the refusal to go back to the source. We want to stay where we are and we cling to ourselves, or we cling to our mother or the earth or to money. Clinging to anything stops our return. Grace is when we open ourselves and allow ourselves to be drawn out of ourselves, to return to God in this movement of love. Sin is always a refusal of love and grace is always a response to love. Love moves the universe as Dante put it, "The love which moves the sun and other stars." The universe comes into being through that motion of love in the Godhead, that spanda or pulse of will, which wishes to express itself in love and in the desire to be loved. God wants to make himself known and he wants us to know him, to return to him in knowledge and love.

In the final state creation and humanity return to God. That movement is taking place and, while sin obstructs it to some extent, redemption overcomes it. Redemption in Christ has overcome the disintegrating forces of sin and has restored mankind to unity. In him we are able to return to the source. We are able to return to God and to exist eternally in God, each participating in the one divine reality, yet remaining distinct. This is the Christian vision. We do not merge in the Godhead like a drop of water into the ocean as is sometimes said, but we enter the Godhead. We are transfigured by God, as Jesus was in the resurrection, and we become one with God, but we do not lose our distinction.

There is a very interesting illustration of what this means in the work of Beatrice Bruteau,[9] where she emphasizes that love is the instinct by which we go out of ourselves to another, and identify ourselves by our participation in another. In doing this we develop and grow. A person is a dynamism of love and we become a person as we give ourselves to others. In other words, we grow by relationship with others. The world is in fact a web of relationships, and each one of us is a centre of relationship. If we isolate ourselves we die; we are breaking the rhythm of the universe and that is sin. On the other hand, if we open ourselves in love we go out to the other. As we relate to another person, when we first encounter them they are an object, but as we begin to know them we begin to share their thoughts, feelings, desires, fears and hopes. We begin to share with one another. Bruteau says that our ultimate desire is to be totally one with that other, so that we share and participate in unity. But this certainly does not mean that we dissolve into the other. Here, as Pierre Teilhard de Chardin emphasizes, "union differentiates." This means that the more we are united with others, the more we become ourselves. So each is in the other and in the One who unites all the others together. The basis of this is the Christian understanding of the Trinity. The Father is in the Son in a total self-giving to the Son, and the "I" of the Son is one with the Father. Similarly, in the Holy Spirit the "I" of the Father and the "I" of the Son are united in the "I" of the Spirit. It is a total interrelationship of unity; in other words, total non-duality and yet with this profound differentiation. That is also what we experience in our lives in the experience of love, when we can share and participate in the identity of the other. The ultimate state is when we all reach that state of pure identity in difference.

A good illustration of this in the Hindu tradition is the "net of Indra," which is a network of pearls so arranged that every pearl reflects every other pearl and the whole of which they are parts. So in the ultimate state each person reflects the One who is present in every person and in everything. This is a total interrelationship of interpenetration and of transparency. These are only words that we use to try to present this mystery to ourselves but they are important because all the time, particularly in India, one is faced with the opposite tendency, which is to think that when one reaches that ultimate state all differences disappear. It is thought that there are no more individuals and no longer a personal God, but only saccidananda, being, knowledge and bliss. That is a profound mystical intuition and Shankara,[10] certainly, realised the unity of all things, but he was not able to reconcile it with differentiation. On the other hand, as we have seen, Kashmir Shaivism, Buddhism and Sufism have all been able to discern how the differentiation is part of the unity. All hold in different ways that the One differentiates himself and yet remains undifferentiated. That is the mystery.

All this has a very practical meaning, which is that our life in this world has eternal value. Each one of us as a person is a unique manifestation of the One, and each has a unique destiny to experience the divine and to experience unity with all the others. It means also that our life in this world day by day, and hour by hour, has eternal value. And it means that history itself, the evolution of humanity and of the world, is all part of this divine drama. The whole universe is to be taken up into the divine along with the whole of humanity in all the stages of its history. All is part of this movement of the divine in matter, in life, in humanity, and we are all being drawn into that, such that our ultimate state is a total fullness of being as we experience the whole.

Again, modern physics affirms that the whole is present in every part. When we begin consciously to enter that state we become aware of ourselves as parts, as it were, of that whole, but also the whole is present in each one of us. Each one is a microcosm, and the macrocosm is present in each one. We are all within that total unity which is ultimately non-dual. This is an absolute unity and yet it embraces all the diversity and all the multiplicity of the universe. It must always be remembered that these are only words which we use to describe a reality infinitely beyond our conception, but they are useful in so far as they point us towards that reality, both theoretically and practically. It is important not least because this affects our practical lives. If we think that the universe is ultimately unreal and that our own lives are unreal we will live accordingly. But it will make all the difference to how we live when we realise that this universe is created by God, that it has infinite eternal value, that each one of us has an infinite eternal value in the sight of God and that we all form a unity which yet embraces all diversity. So we are fulfilled in that Absolute in our own individual being, and in the whole cosmic order and the fullness of Reality.[11]

From *The Golden String*:

In the palæolithic caves which have been discovered in the south of France it has been found that there are long winding passages leading from the front of the cave by a difficult and often dangerous path into the inmost recesses of the rock, and there in the darkness of the interior are to be found those drawings of animals which astonish us with their power and beauty. Why was it that these pictures were drawn in the darkness of the interior where they could only be seen by the light of a torch of moss dipped in animal fat? Miss Rachel Levy in her *Gate of Horn* has given us the answer. The pictures on the wall were sacred images by means of which it was believed that man could enter into communion with the divine powers, and the long, winding difficult passage to the interior represented the dark and difficult approach to the divine mystery.

We find this symbolism continued all through Neolithic times, in the megalithic temples and in the ritual dances of primitive peoples today; always there is the laborious approach to the sacred place where the encounter with the divine mystery is to take place. But it is in the Egyptian Pyramids that the full significance of this symbolism is revealed. In the interior of the Pyramid there is a long winding stairway with many twists and turns by which it was intended that the Pharaoh should make his ascent to the summit, and on the walls were depicted the scenes of the Pharaoh's journey through the underworld. Here it becomes clear that the winding passage is the path of man's ascent to God, and this path is a journey through the realms of death leading to the place where man ascends above this world and enters into immortality.

Thus from the earliest times, of which we have any knowledge, it seems to have been understood that our life in this world is a journey towards God. The journey is from the mouth of the cave, which represents the external world, into the interior which appears as darkness; it is the passage from the outer to the inner world. It is this journey which is represented by the descent of Aeneas into the underworld in search of his Father. The same motive appears in the Odyssey as the return of the Hero by a long and difficult voyage home, where his wife awaits him. Or again it is found in the legend of Theseus making his way to the centre of the Labyrinth in search of his Bride.

All these stories are symbols of the same mystery of the search for God which is at the same time the return to our true home. It is represented sometimes as a new birth, a return to the womb, or again as a descent into the tomb by which we rise again to a new life. Always it has been understood that our life in this world, as Keats said, is a "perpetual allegory"; everything has meaning only in reference to something beyond. We are, as Plato saw it, like men in a cave who see reality reflected on the walls of the cave, as in a cinema. The illusion of this world is that by which we mistake the figures on the screen for reality. This is the sin of idolatry, for idolatry is nothing but the worship of images, the mistaking the image of truth for Truth itself.

Scientific materialism in the modern world is the precise counterpart of pagan idolatry in the ancient world; it is the substitution of appearance for reality. For science as such is only concerned with phenomena, that is, with things as they appear to the senses: its function is, in the Greek phrase, to "save the phenomena," to account for the appearance of things. But of the reality which underlies the appearance, of the real nature of things, science can give us no knowledge at all. We only begin to awake to reality when we realize that the material world, the world of space and time, as it appears to our senses, is nothing but a sign and a symbol of a mystery which infinitely transcends it. That is why the images in the palæolithic cave were painted in the dark; it is only when we have passed beyond the world of images that we can enter into communion with the mystery which lies beyond.

This sense of mystery transcending the world, of which this world, as we know it, is only a sign, is the root of all religion. It underlies the religion of primitive man; it is embodied in the ancient myths and legends; it is found at the basis both of Egyptian and Babylonian religion, and it takes shape finally in the mystery religions which are found all over the ancient world. In these religions the cycle of life and death in nature, the passage of the seasons through the death of winter to rebirth in the spring, is seen as a symbol of man's passage through death into life, of his rebirth to immortality.

In the great awakening which took place in so many different parts of the world in the first millennium before Christ, which Karl Jaspers called the "axial period" of human history, the full significance of this religion comes to light. It was then that as by a kind of universal awakening the real meaning of life seems to have dawned upon the human mind. In India and China, in Persia and in Greece, a movement of thought began, by which mankind finally pierced through the barrier of the senses and discovered the mystery of the world which lies beyond. This was the great discovery which brought enlightenment to the Buddha; this was the source of the inspiration of the Upanishads and the tradition of the Vedanta: this was what was revealed in China as the Tao and in Greece as the Logos.

To each people the mystery was revealed in a different way. To the Indian it came rather as sense of the utter unreality of the phenomenal world in comparison with the reality of that which lay beyond. To the Chinese it appeared as a principle of harmony, a cosmic order uniting man and nature in an organic society. The Greek saw it as a law of Reason by which "all things are steered through all things," which gave rise to Plato's conception of the "world of ideas" and to Plotinus's vision of the One, transcending all thought and all being.

Thus from the beginning of the world, as far as we can judge, man has known himself to be in the presence of a mystery. He has expressed his sense of the mystery in myth and legend; he has striven to approach the mystery by prayer and sacrifice; he has tried to apprehend it by thought. But at a certain point in history the mystery chose to reveal itself. It manifested itself by signs and wonders to a particular people; it declared its will through the voice of the Prophets. It was revealed as a Person whose will is justice and whose nature is love. It appeared on earth in a human nature and revealed in that human nature the destiny to which man had through all centuries aspired. For Christ came to recapitulate all the stages of human history, to sum up in himself the destiny of mankind. It was no accident that he was born in a cave. He travelled the whole of that long, difficult and laborious path like Aeneas into the underworld; he passed through death into life; he ascended above this world of space and time into the divine presence.

But Christ did not open this path for himself alone. On the day before he was to die, he instituted a rite by which his disciples might be enabled to follow him on the same path by which he had traveled. He took bread and wine, the symbols of sacrifice throughout the ancient world, and made them the sacramental means by which his disciples might share in the mystery of his death and enter into a new life with him.[12]

Trappist Martyrs of Tibhirine, Algeria (d. 1996)

Seek peace and pursue it. (RB, Prologue 17)

Stability unto death. Seven Trappist monks—Father Christian Marie de Chergé, who served his community as Prior; Brother Luke Dochier; Father Christopher Lebreton; Brother Paul Favre Miville; Father Bruno Lemarchand; Brother Michael Fleury; and Father Celestine Ringeard—chose to remain with their Muslim neighbors in Tibhirine through a ruthlessly violent civil war with its escalating violence, sealing that friendship with their lifeblood.

The village of Tibhirine is located in the Atlas Mountains of northern Algeria, an African nation on the Mediterranean Sea. Algeria had been wracked with civil war and armed violence for years, yet Tibhirine was known as an oasis of peace and friendship between Christian and Muslim neighbors. The monks had established this monastery, called Notre Dame de l'Atlas (Our Lady of Atlas), in 1934, with a desire to witness to peace and to be a Christian presence in a predominantly Muslim nation.

In monastic profession, Benedictines promise stability to a group of fellow monastics and to the people of the local region in which the monastery is situated. Throughout history, monastic communities have been confronted with the reality of war, terrorism, and death. Each monastery in its own time has discerned the call of the Holy Spirit when deciding whether to stay with the local people or to go into exile as a community. As violence increased in Algeria, and particularly as threats against the monks of Tibhirine continued, the community discerned the call of the Holy Spirit to remain with their neighbors. They chose to live out stability unto death.

For the monastic community, the decision to stay in Tibhirine with their Muslim neighbors was not a sudden and rash one. On Christmas

Eve, 1993, they were visited by six armed men who were members of the armed insurgency fighting the Algerian military. The insurgents came to coerce the monks to support them financially, strategically, and medically. The armed insurgents also offered armed guards to protect the monastery. After prayerful communal discussion and several rounds of votes, the monks refused to grant them any assistance other than medical help administered at the monastery. The monks refused the offer of protection and also refused to move to a protected area, insisting on remaining in their monastery. The monks would live in peace with their neighbors, and would not take sides in the civil war.

The monks understood the seriousness of their situation and of their decision to remain in Tibhirine. If any monk needed to leave the monastery he could not return, and the community no longer accepted novices until the civil war was over. The monks placed their lives and the future of their monastic foundation into God's providential care.

Each December, the monks renewed the commitment among themselves to remain in Tibhirine. Offers had been extended for the monks to move to a safer location, but they remained prayerfully convinced that they were living where God desired them. Armed insurgents continued to be seen in their region. Other religious in Algeria had been assassinated, but many communities chose to remain and continue their peaceful Christian witness. The monks of Tibhirine, as a community, continued in their conviction despite increasing threats.

Benedict reminds his followers to "keep your eye on death every day" (RB 4:47), affirming with them that "we will never depart from his [God's] teaching and we will persevere in his doctrine in the monastery until death. Likewise, we will participate in the passion of Christ through patience so as to deserve to be companions in God's kingdom" (Prologue 50). Seven monks were kidnapped on March 27, 1996, and held captive. The Armed Islamic Group (GIA) demanded the release of political prisoners held by the Algerian and French governments, in exchange for the lives of the monks. The monks were beheaded on May 21, 1996. They are buried in the cemetery of their beloved monastery.

From a letter written by Father Christian de Cherge to Sayah Attiyah, chief of the Armed Islamic Group who had come to their monastery on Christmas Eve 1993:

> Brother, allow me to address you like this, as man to man, believer to believer. . . . In the present conflict in which our country is

engaged it seems impossible for us to take sides. The fact that we are foreigners forbids it. Our state as monks (*ruhbân*) binds us to the choice God has made for us, which is a life of prayer, simplicity, manual work, hospitality and sharing with everyone, especially with the poor. . . . These essential qualities of our life have been chosen freely by each one of us. They bind us until death. I do not think that it is the will of God that this death should come to us through you. . . . If one day the Algerians state that we are not welcome, we will respect their desire to see us leave, although we would regret it deeply. I know that we will continue to love them ALL, and that includes you as one of them. When and how will this message reach you? It doesn't matter! I needed to write it to you today. Forgive me for having done it in my mother tongue. You will understand me. And the ONE Creator of all life lead us! AMIN![1]

From *Testament of Father Christian* (opened on Pentecost Sunday, May 26, 1996)

When we face an A-DIEU . . .

If it should happen one day—and it could be today—that I become a victim of the terrorism which now seems ready to engulf all the foreigners living in Algeria, I would like my community, my Church and my family to remember that my life was GIVEN to God and to this country. I ask them to accept that fact that the One Master of all life was not a stranger to this brutal departure. I would ask them to pray for me: for how could I be found worthy of such an offering? I ask them to associate this death with so many other equally violent ones which are forgotten through indifference or anonymity.

My life has no more value than any other. Nor any less value. In any case, it has not the innocence of childhood. I have lived long enough to know that I am an accomplice in the evil which seems, alas, to prevail in the world, even in the evil which might blindly strike me down. I would like, when the time comes, to have a moment of spiritual clarity which would allow me to beg forgiveness of God and of my fellow human beings, and at the same time forgive with all my heart the one who will strike me down.

I could not desire such a death. It seems to me important to state this. I do not see, in fact, how I could rejoice if the people I love were indiscriminately accused of my murder. It would be too high a price to pay for what will perhaps be called the "grace of martyrdom" to owe this to an Algerian, whoever he may be, especially if he says he is acting in fidelity to what he believes to be Islam. I am aware of the scorn which can be heaped on the Algerians indiscriminately. I am also aware of the caricatures of Islam which a certain Islamism fosters. It is too easy to soothe one's conscience by identifying this religious way with the fundamentalist ideology of its extremists. For me, Algeria and Islam are not that, but rather a body and a soul. I have proclaimed this often enough, I think, in the light of what I have received from it. I so often find there that true strand of the Gospel which I learned at my mother's knee, my very first Church, precisely in Algeria, and already inspired with respect for Muslim believers.

Obviously, my death will appear to confirm those who hastily judged me naïve or idealistic: "Let him tell us now what he thinks of it!" But these persons would know that finally my most avid curiosity will be set free. This is what I shall be able to do, please God: immerse my gaze in that of the Father to contemplate with him His children of Islam just as he sees them, all shining with the glory of Christ, the fruit of His Passion, filled with the Gift of the Spirit whose secret joy will always be to establish communion and restore the likeness, playing with the differences.

For this life lost, totally mine and totally theirs, for the sake of that JOY in everything and in spite of everything. In this THANK YOU, which is said for everything in my life from now on, I certainly include you, friends of yesterday and today and you, my friends of this place, along with my mother and father, my sisters and brothers and their families. You are the hundredfold granted as was promised!

And also you, my last-minute friend, who will not have known what you were doing: Yes, I want this THANK YOU and this "A-DIEU" to be for you, too, because in God's face I see yours.

May we meet again as happy thieves in Paradise, if it please God, the Father of us both.

AMEN! IN H'ALLAH!
Tibhirine, January 1, 1994

Christian+[2]

From the "testimony" of Bernardo Olivera given at the funeral of the seven monks of Tibhirine

What can a monk say about his brother monks? I know, as they did, that our charism in the Church is to be silent, work, intercede and praise God. But we know, too, that there are times to speak, as there are times to keep silence.

The hidden voice of the monks remained silently in the cloisters of Our Lady of Atlas for more than fifty years. This voice was changed during the last two months into a cry of love which has echoed in the hearts of millions of believers and persons of good will. Our seven brothers of Tibhirine—Christian, Luke, Christopher, Michael, Bruno, Celestine and Paul—are transformed today into spokesmen for all those stifled voices and unknown persons who have given their life for a more humane world. Our seven monks lend their voice to me, too, today.

The monks's testimony, like that of every believing Christian, can only be understood as a prolongation of the testimony of Christ himself. Our life following Christ should manifest with total clarity the divine liberality of the good news of the gospel which we desire to live. This good news is that a life given and offered is never lost. It is always found again in Him who is the Life.

We must enter into the world of the other, whether that person be Christian or Muslim. In fact if the "other" does not exist as such, there is no space for true love. We need to be disturbed and enriched by the existence of the other. Let us remain open and sensitive to every voice that challenges us. Let us choose love, forgiveness and communion against every form of hatred, vengeance and violence. Let us believe without flinching in the deep desire for peace which resides in the depth of every human heart.

Our brother monks are a ripe fruit of this Church which is living the paschal mystery in Algeria. Our brother monks are also a ripe fruit of this people of Algeria who received them and esteemed their life during these many years of presence and communion. For this reason, I want to express a word of thanks on our part to all of you. Church of Algeria, all you Algerians, adorers of the one God: a heartfelt thank you for the respect and love you have shown for our brother monks.

Listen, if you can possibly listen:
To come to Him is to leave oneself.
Silence: up there is the world of vision.
For them, our monks of Tibhirine, the word is only
Seeing.
Amen.[3]

Benedictines and the Chant Tradition

And let us stand to sing in such a way that our mind is in harmony with our voice. (RB 19:7)

When people refer to chant, most often they mean Benedictine chant. Chant is a form of sacred song that has been with us for centuries. However, chant is not strictly Christian. It is found in most cultures and most religious traditions.

In the Christian tradition, chant is sung in unison, normally unaccompanied, following a single melody line. Usually the chanted texts are from Sacred Scripture, especially the Psalms, or poetic texts reflecting on Scripture or expressing Christian theology.[1] Over the centuries, different styles of chant emerged in different cultural contexts (Ambrosian in northern Italy, Gallican in Gaul, Mozarabic in the Iberian Peninsula, Old Roman and Gregorian). The Christian East has its own ancient chant tradition.

This chapter focuses primarily on the chant tradition in the West as preserved and perpetuated by Benedictines. While chant is prayer that is best evoked from the heart, Benedictines have a long tradition of choirs who practice the techniques of chant and vocal control. There is a desire to balance the aesthetic beauty of chant with the prayer of chant. Vocal styles vary across cultures and throughout history, but Benedictines strive for beauty as well as prayerfulness.

Chant

While the earliest adherents to the Christian movement certainly sang songs and hymns during their gatherings, singing of Old Testament Psalms rarely occurred before the third century. Newly composed hymns were preferred, until the popularity of some heretical hymns[2] led liturgical leaders to find other sources for hymnody.

The women and men dwelling in the monasteries of the desert and city established through their common practice what would become the core of the Monastic Office, namely the continuous recitation or chanting of the full book of Psalms.[3] The psalms and much of Sacred Scripture were memorized. Thus the office could be chanted privately or together with other monastics or while busy with manual labor. With time and a desire to emulate the venerated desert ascetics[4] who prayed without ceasing, more and more urban Christians aspired to pray the full psalmody.

Styles for singing the psalms, either in Divine Office or at Eucharist, took no structured form for several centuries. Early chant, commonly called Old Roman chant, preceded the Gregorian chant we are familiar with today. Gregorian chant was developed not during the time of Gregory I (590–604), but by the *schola cantorum* under Pope Vitalian (657–672).[5] Old Roman chant was monotonous and somewhat formulaic, with a melody line that did not necessarily match the sung text. Gregorian chant was freer flowing, precise and definitive, with a melody line that more accurately served the text and an ornate oscillating style that is pleasing to the ear. Choirs and cantors memorized both text and chant instruction. The chant tradition, in its earliest centuries, relied on the chant master's memory. Sometimes this worked and sometimes it did not. While variations are humanly natural, certain chants or styles suffered.

What we today call plainchant is closer to Gregorian chant. It retains the light beauty of Gregorian chant without the burden of technical detail. Gregorian chant, sung well, is technically challenging and requiring both mental and vocal skill. Plainchant often uses the same melody for various texts. This is quite typical for the ordinary psalmody in which the same psalm tone is used for all the verses of a psalm. Yet it is also used for the more complicated psalm forms such as in the case of the Office antiphons. In plainchant effort is made to adapt the melody to the rhythmical structure of differing texts, and oftentimes it can be observed that care is taken to bring out the sentiments of the words.

Rather than collecting commentary on chant, this chapter traces the history of chant in the Benedictine tradition, highlighting the place of chant in liturgy.

Pope St. Gregory the Great (540–604)

Gregory was born into a wealthy patrician family with estates around Italy and Sicily. He grew up in a time of turmoil as Rome was sacked,

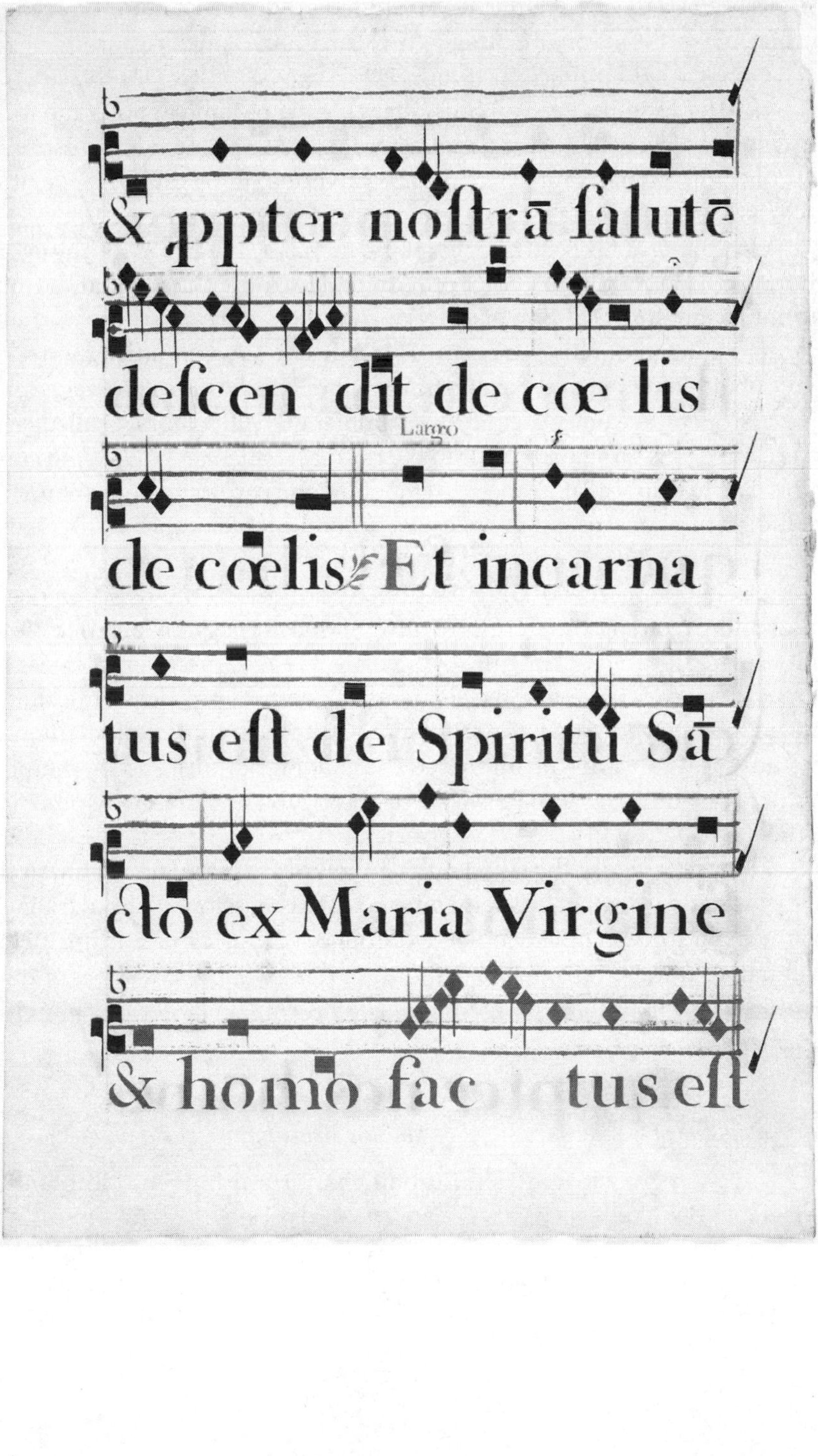
& ꝓpter noſtrā ſalutē
deſcen dit de cœ lis
Largo
de cœlis Et incarna
tus eſt de Spiritū Sā
cto ex Maria Virgine
& homo fac tus eſt

garrisoned, and then abandoned repeatedly. Well educated and renowned for his keen intellect, his education included grammar, rhetoric, dialectic, and legal studies. From a young age, he meditated on Scripture.

Gregory held public office, and by 573 he was prefect for the city of Rome. After long prayer and inner struggle, he became a monk the following year. He established a monastery named St. Andrew at his residence on the Cælian Hill in Rome and converted his Sicilian estates into monasteries.

Gregory and his followers lived the monastic life in the tradition of this unknown monk, Benedict of Nursia. He knew the reputation for holiness and spiritual power surrounding Benedict and drew on this reputation to create his *Dialogues*. The only sources of information we have about Benedict and Scholastica are the *Rule* and these *Dialogues*.

As a cleric at Rome, Gregory was familiar with its pastoral challenges. The church was growing and faced the normal challenges of clashing cultures. Political upheaval, changes in emperors, and corruption in the church, had direct impact upon the believing community. Gregory poured his grand energies into supporting the church in every way possible.

Elected pope in 590, Gregory directly addressed the need for pastoral reform among the clergy, inspiring hope among the laity. He also addressed significant liturgical concerns. He is remembered as "the Great" for recognizing that the elements of good liturgy, including singing and chant, were a major concern for the Christian community. Among the liturgical concerns, he improved the chant repertoire and its performance for both the Roman Office of the churches and the Monastic Office.

Pope St. Gregory the Great was canonized by popular acclamation shortly after his death. He is remembered for his passion in popularizing chant and improving the people's experience of music in the liturgy. He committed limited resources to providing this skill to the reaches of the Empire. The chant that emerged in his day is called Gregorian chant in his memory.

St. Augustine of Canterbury (d. 604) and the Benedictines of England

Pope Gregory introduced Roman chant traditions into England. Venerable Bede tells us in his *Ecclesiastical History of the English Peoples* of Pope Gregory's chance encounter with English slaves in the slave market in Rome. Around the same time, word reached Rome that pagan inhabitants of Britain were ready to embrace the Christian faith if preachers and teachers would be sent to them. The pope decided to send about forty of his monks, naming the Prior of St. Andrew's, St. Augustine of Canterbury, to lead this missionary endeavor to Britain. The band departed in June 596.

After a long journey wracked with self-doubt and the difficulties of establishing good relationships with kings and rulers, Augustine and his companions arrived in Britain and were invited to establish their home in the royal capital of Canterbury. These forty monks continued a routine of monastic life and began preaching and teaching in their host nation.

Both Augustine and the local king insisted on religious freedom; no one was forced or compelled to convert to Christianity. Pope Gregory had granted Augustine the freedom to adopt any practices from among the local believers that supported and nurtured their faith. However, Augustine preferred Roman orderliness. Having been trained in the Roman chant and ecclesiastical hymn tradition, he and his companions introduced these chants and hymns into Britain. The monks successfully integrated the Roman tradition with native chants.

Pope Gregory sent Bishop Paulinus to Britain as reinforcement for Augustine. The people of England had favorably received the Benedictine monks with their gifts of education and culture. A great demand for more monks, priests, and bishops persisted. Double monasteries, monastic communities with houses for women and for men, were being established in major centers, bringing learning, libraries, chant, the arts, and artisan's skills (farming techniques, book copying, animal husbandry, etc.) to the region. James the Deacon was sent to York in 633 to continue teaching the chant tradition.

Bishop St. Theodore of Canterbury (d. 690) was a Benedictine monk trained in Rome and made Archbishop of Canterbury (669–690). His liturgical training as a Benedictine monk served as his model in England. He tirelessly traveled Britain and sought to improve the quality of worship. His successor, Bishop Wilfrid (d. 709), originally a monk of Lindisfarne, sent Stephen Aeddi north from Kent to teach the churches ecclesiastical chant.

Abbot Benedict Bishop (d. 689), Venerable Bede's mentor and founding Abbot of Wearmouth and Jarrow, desired to improve the quality of church singing and chant; he also wanted to conform their liturgical practices to those that he experienced in Rome. He brought back with him the arch-cantor John, who served both in the schola cantorum of St. Peter's in the Vatican as well as St. Martin's, a monastery attached to

St. Peter's. John was valued for being an expert in both church chant and monastic chant. Abbot John taught the order and procedures of singing and techniques for public proclamation of sacred texts (today called lectoring). He also created copies of chant texts and other texts for the celebration of feast days throughout the liturgical year. Venerable Bede tells us that John's manuscripts were further copied and dispersed throughout the realm.

Saxon Benedictine missionaries brought the tradition of Gregorian Chant into Germany, understanding that Christian conversion needed the support of Christian culture. These English Benedictine monastics included St. Boniface (d. 754), St. Leoba (710–782), St. Walburga (710–777), and others.

Emperor Charlemagne (or Charles the Great) (742–814)

Charles the Great ruled an unwieldy empire, from 768 until his death. In later years, he was determined to bring liturgical conformity to his Empire in the West. While his motives were undoubtedly complex, liturgical conformity ended conflict over "the right way" to chant the Divine Office or celebrate Eucharist. Conformity also strengthened his power base in the Empire. Charlemagne did have a good background in music and liturgy and an honest desire to see that church services were the best that they could possibly be. Charlemagne required all monasteries to adopt the Rule of Benedict and to accept the tradition of Gregorian chant. He also provided personnel and resources (copies of chant books) for the major ecclesiastical centers so that local choirs could be trained. Chant books found their way into ecclesiastical and monastic libraries, where further copies could be made. As a result of Charlemagne's edict, chant notation found in manuscripts from the ninth century forward, and those in staff notation from the eleventh to the fourteenth century, are quite uniform.

Chant was originally memorized and relied too heavily upon fragile memories. As chant spread throughout the empire, and especially with Charlemagne's edicts, chant began to be written down. A uniformity of chant tradition was preserved. Understanding the intentions of the original chant master was imperative because one needed to understand what was originally expressed by the neumatic notation. Neumes are dots, hooks, and small strokes that provide the general up and down pattern of the melody. However, neumes neither indicate the tonal pitch nor how long to hold the note. They were useful to individual choir masters, but could not be passed down effectively.

Scholar Katharine Le Mée points out that between the ninth and eleventh centuries, Benedictine music theorists such as Aurelian, Hucbald, Pseudo-Odo, and Hermannus Contractus applied mathematical theory to the art of chant.[6] Included in their contributions were adaptations of Greek modes to create a modal system for use with the chant of the West.

Guido d'Arezzo (ca. 995–1050)

Guido was educated by the Benedictines and entered monastic life at St. Maur des Fosses near Paris. Immersed in the chant tradition and the challenges of copying and training others in its notation, he began looking for better ways to record and transmit this tradition. There was no uniformity in the method and meaning of chant notation. Unless the cantor knew the patterns of notation used by the chant master who created a text, the chant text might prove undecipherable. He wanted to find a way to make chant notation easily understood and taught, so that monks would be able to pick up and sing the chant straight from a text.

Guido's innovations were not popular. His fellow monks fought against learning a new way to read chant texts. Life became so difficult that Guido moved to the Benedictine monastery of Pomposa near Ferrara, Italy. Here he continued to work at improving his new system of musical notation with the same response of rejection, anger, and strife. Guido finally asked for permission to transfer his promise of stability to the Camaldolese monastery at Arezzo. Here he perfected a new system of notation that provided clarity and order.

At the invitation of Pope John XIX (1024–1033), Guido visited Rome in 1028 to teach the pope, the Roman clergy, and singers his new form of notation. He was well received; experienced singers were surprised and delighted at the ease with which they were able to read and learn the melodies without assistance from a chant master. He was invited to remain, but the Roman climate did not agree with his health and he returned to his monastery at Arezzo.

Each and every time any of us pick up a hymnal or a book of praise for Liturgy of the Hours, we benefit from Guido's genius. Chant was originally memorized and only a chant master understood the musical notations on a page. These notations were complex and merely indicated to the choir director the shapes to be traced in the air. The gestures were supposed to remind the schola or choir of the melody that they had already memorized and establish rhythm.[7] Scholars agree that it took several years (Guido said ten years) for a student to learn the traditional chant repertory.

Guido created four permanent staff lines and utilized the spaces between the lines (today we say half-steps). He indicated, by combining the letters of the alphabet with the neumatic signs, the various intervals of the melody as well as its rhythm. His system is called staff notation. Four lines were all that was needed for the range of Gregorian melodies. There have been adaptations of Guido's initial genius, in part because not all Gregorian chant fit neatly into his hexachords (six-note sequences), or into the original system of eight modes.

Guido advocated the utilization of contrary movement of voices, meaning that the upper ascended while the other descended, rather than the traditional pattern where both parts moved in the same direction. This significantly contributed to the development of sacred polyphony that would become prominent in the centuries to come.

By the thirteenth century, the neumes of Gregorian chant were usually written in square notation on a staff with four lines and three spaces and a clef marker. In square notation, small groups of ascending notes on a syllable are shown as stacked squares, read from bottom to top, while descending notes are written with diamonds read from left to right. In melismatic chants, in which a syllable may be sung to a large number of notes, a series of smaller groups of neumes are written in succession, read from left to right. Special neumes such as the oriscus, quilisma, and liquescent neumes, indicate particular vocal treatments for these notes.

Abbess Hildegard of Bingen (1098–1179)

Abbess Hildegard of Bingen was a creative genius. She composed hymns and antiphons, new chants for the psalms, and vocal settings for liturgical texts. Monastic chant in her day had become deep and heavy, favoring male voices. She found it burdensome for her sisters to sing. Joy was the hallmark of the monastic observance and she felt that the chant she and her sisters had been taught drained that joy from the experience of Divine Office.

Hildegard created a new form of chant for her sisters that was light and airy and free. Yet its freedom served a purpose and supported a text. Her chant was also quite difficult and demanded rigorous lungpower. At times her vocal range was two and a half octaves. Her intent was to make the experience of Divine Office a delight and joy for her sisters.

Hildegard wrote chant melody and text that expressed her powerful visions and understanding of the divine as revealed through her visions. Her songs reveal the feminine face of God and Holy Wisdom, a feminine image, while remaining grounded in the traditional theology of her day.

With the resurgence of interest in Hildegard, much of her music has been recorded and is available for enjoyment and meditation.

In the Aftermath of the French Revolution and the European Secularization

The French Revolution and Napoleon's conquests were violent. Churches and monasteries were burned; priests and nuns were executed, imprisoned, or sent into exile. The French government sought to marginalize and control the church. Beginning in 1792, the French and other European governments instituted laws of secularization that suppressed monasteries and other forms of religious life. Those monasteries still in existence were denied the right to accept new members, with the intention of taking away the land once the last members died out. Other monasteries were driven underground or their members moved out of continental Europe to Great Britain or North America. The French secularization laws were modified in 1830, but the French government continued its harassment of monasteries into the twentieth century.

Solesmes, France

In 1832 the French Benedictine Abbey of St. Pierre at Solesmes was re-established by Dom Prosper Guéranger (1805–1875), a diocesan priest. The men's community at Solesmes had been suppressed during the Revolution and its monks had fled to the Isle of Wight. The French government sold the land and buildings to Guéranger. He and a few like-minded friends began living the Benedictine life, making their monastic profession in Rome. His passions were to see the restoration of the Divine Office, to foster liturgical renewal in France and to support serious scholarly study of plainchant and the early development of the Mass. He wanted to form the laity along with monastics.

Prayer for the laity in France had become a conglomeration of individualistic, extra-liturgical devotions centered on the Blessed Sacrament, Marian prayers, the rosary, and other devotions. This had the effect of rendering the celebration of Mass secondary, and the Divine Office nearly obsolete for the laity. Guéranger sought to restore a meaningful sacramental theology and liturgical spirituality in the lives of ordinary believers.

Guéranger wrote a three volume series, *Institutions liturgiques* (1840, 1841, 1851), a comprehensive history of the liturgy from the patristic era to his day. Hoping to entice the laity into a practice of daily prayer grounded in the liturgy, he began a multi-volume series entitled *The Liturgical Year* (1841), which was a meditative commentary on the prayers of the liturgy and the Divine Office of each day throughout the year. His hope was to deepen comprehension of liturgical texts and scripture, offering deeper meaning to the laity attending Mass and Divine Office.

Guéranger was the first to use the expression, the "liturgical movement." He wrote in 1851:

> Let us hope that the liturgical movement which is expanding and spreading will awaken also among the faithful the meaning of the Divine Office, that their attendance at it in church will become more intelligent, and that the time will come when, once more imbued with the spirit of the liturgy, they will feel the need to participate in the sacred chants.[8]

The liturgical movement (approximately 1833–1963) essentially began with the vision and passion of Guéranger and his fellow monks at Solesmes. Their vision of a liturgical renewal that encompassed every aspect of Christian life, including chant in Mass and the Divine Office, and which was to include the full laity, would sweep across Christendom.

Around 1860 Dom Guéranger assigned two of his monks, Dom Jausions (1834–1870) and Dom Pothier (1835–1923), to make a thorough examination of the codices of chant and to compile a gradual for the monastery. Their twenty-three years of careful work resulted in the *Liber Gradualis*, the first serious attempt to return to the purity of Gregorian chant. After its completion, a committed school of critical research under Dom Mocquereau was established. One significant result of their work was *Paléographie Musicale*, a series of publications that provided photographic reproductions of the principal manuscripts of plainchant along with scholarly discussions of these texts. In 1903 they published the *Liber Usualis*, an extract from the gradual and antiphonary, which included some melodic improvements and valuable rhythmical directions.

Abbess Cécile Bruyère (1845–1909) established the women's Benedictine monastery, Sainte-Cécile, in Solesmes in 1866. A friend and student of Dom Guéranger, Abbess Cécile was a gifted spiritual director and monastery administrator. While a recognized master of the spiritual life, she was equally balanced and grounded and practical in the ordering of monastic life. When the monks were expelled from their monastery by the French military, it was her calm presence that eased arrangements for the monks to move into private homes.[9] In 1885 she published *The Spiritual Life and Prayer*. The nuns were serious students of chant as well as the spiritual life. To this day the Divine Office chanted by the nuns is renowned.

Building upon the work instigated by the monks at Solesmes, Pope Pius X issued *Motu proprio: Tra le sollecitudini* in 1903, which called for a reform of church music. In addition, the pope called for a return to Gregorian chant as recovered by the monks of Solesmes with the express hope that the laity would more fully participate in the liturgy. He commanded that the traditional form of plainchant be introduced into all churches as soon as possible.

Beuron, Germany

Maurus Wolter (1825–1890), a diocesan priest, had entered St. Paul-Outside-the-Walls, an ancient Benedictine Abbey in Rome, in 1856. His brother, Placidus (1828–1908), also a diocesan priest, had already joined this monastery. Another brother, Hildebrand, joined them as well. The brothers, like others, had hoped that a restored and rejuvenated Benedictine observance would help to restore Catholic Culture in Europe.

Pope Pius IX appointed Maurus spiritual director to Princess Katherine of Hohenzollern-Sigmaringen. In 1863 the princess offered Wolter the old Augustinian Abbey of Beuron, in the Danube valley in Germany. Placidus joined Maurus in restoring the Abbey, and their monastic model was the Abbey of Solesmes.

Maurus Wolter lived at Solesmes for some months, where he studied and imbued the Solesmes spirit. The first Beuron novice also studied at Solesmes. Later the Abbot of Solesmes sent one of their members to be novice master at Beuron.

In 1875, the German government exiled the monks of Beuron for twelve years. Through practical need and a desire to reintroduce Benedictine life where it had been banished in centuries past, the monks of Beuron established new communities. An abbey was established at Maredsous in Belgium in 1872, with Placidus Wolter as its first superior. He continued the work of liturgical research. Dom von Caloen, rector of the abbey school, published the first French-Latin Missal in 1882. The monks of Maredsous, intimately involved in the liturgical movement and the Eucharistic Congresses, remained dedicated to serious scholarly work that supported a deep interior life. The monks established the

Messager des fideles, later named *Revue Benedictine*, which is still in publication.

On the death of Maurus in 1890, Placidus succeeded him as archabbot of Beuron. He remained in that position until 1908, tirelessly promoting a return to a rigorous monastic observance and a high standard of liturgical life. Placidus was instrumental in giving support to the Beuronese school of religious painting and sculpture under such monastic artists as Desiderius Lenz (1832–1928) and Gabriel Wüger (d. 1892), which can be seen in many churches and monasteries around the world.

Abbey of Maria Laach, Germany

The Benedictine Abbey of Maria Laach was originally established in 1093 and suppressed in 1802. In 1892 monks from Beuron were able to return and reestablish monastic life there. The abbey, especially under the influence of Dom Odo Casel (1886–1948) and Abbot Ildefons Herwegen (1874–1946) was the center of major liturgical scholarship in Germany.

Ildefons Herwegen, abbot from 1913 to 1946, was the author of thirty books and major articles. He established the Institute of Liturgical and Monastic Studies at Maria Laach (1931) and served as editor of *Ecclesia Orans*. To this day, the abbey of Maria Laach is a major center of liturgical art.

Odo Casel was part of the movement in Catholic theology that had begun with Johann Adam Mohler in Germany and John Henry Newman in England. They had recovered the idea that the church is a spiritual and organic union in Christ rather than an authoritarian or legalistic institution. Through Casel's influence the Eucharist and the whole liturgy of the church came to be recognized as the efficacious memorial of the mystery of Christ's death and resurrection, offered by the whole corporate body of worshipers through the power of the Holy Spirit.

Dom Casel wrote *The Mystery of Christian Worship*, which was to influence the thinking of the liturgical movement in the first decades of the nineteenth century. He expanded his approach in the fifteen volumes he edited of *Jahrbuch für Liturgiewissenschaft* (1921–1941). He presented the sacraments as mysteries, internal actions of Christ. Casel devoted himself to the theology of liturgy. His major theological contribution was to establish the centrality of the paschal mystery to Christian worship.

From 1922 until his death, Dom Casel was chaplain to the Benedictine nuns at Herstelle. The psalms of the Divine Office had been replaced with eucharistic devotional prayers and perpetual adoration of the

Blessed Sacrament.[10] He dedicated his years as chaplain leading the nuns back to a deep appreciation of the Divine Office, chant, and the Benedictine tradition. This gave legitimacy and impetus to the desires of the American Benedictine sisters to be restored to that privilege.

Mont César, Belgium

A foundation from Maredsous, Mont César, was located in the midst of the ancient Catholic University in Louvain. One of its most famous members was Dom Columba Marmion (1858–1923), who was instrumental in bringing elements of the liturgical movement to women religious and the laity. Another was Dom Lambert Beauduin (1873–1960), who was considered responsible for bringing the liturgical movement to Belgium. As professor at Sant'Anselmo in Rome, he heavily influenced the American students there. He also played a significant role in the birth of the ecumenical movement.

Beauduin presented an address, "The Full Prayer of the Church," in which he called for the active participation of the people in the work of the church, especially the liturgy. The unique characteristics of his approach were that it called for the active participation of the laity and was based on parochial ministry outside the monastery. His approach translated theoretical ideas into popular language and used mass media elements, publications, and conferences to motivate people and disseminate ideas.

A saying attributed to Beauduin encapsulates his passion: "What a shame that the liturgy remains the endowment of an elite; we are aristocrats of the liturgy; all people should be able to nourish themselves from it, even the simplest people: We must democratize the liturgy."[11]

In each of these monastic centers, revival of chant was foundational to other liturgical work. These monasteries copied and preserved chant manuscripts and sources. They established and maintained a dedicated professional approach to chant as the foundation of liturgy.

The United States

Virgil Michel (1888–1938) of Saint John's Abbey in Collegeville, MN, studied at the Benedictine University of Sant'Anselmo in Rome, where Beaudoin introduced him to the scholarly chant work accomplished in Europe. He spent time at Solesmes learning chant technique and became familiar with the liturgical movement. On his return to Saint John's

Abbey, Abbot Alcuin Deutsch supported the beginnings of an American liturgical movement by establishing the magazine *Orate Fratres* (later *Worship*). He began the Liturgical Press, and with it "The Popular Liturgical Library," a series of pastoral liturgical works.

Very early on, the liturgical movement in the United States would have far more practical, pastoral, and social aspects to its expression than Europe, which was more intellectual and scholarly. The liturgical movement in the United States was closely connected with social issues and movements like the Catholic Worker Movement and "Catholic Action."

In 1926 the full celebration of the Divine Office was restored to the Benedictine women of the United States. When Benedictine women came to the United States from Europe, they had intended to continue their tradition of praying the Divine Office with their missionary endeavors. Much to their horror, Abbot Boniface Wimmer (d. 1887) made arrangements with the Holy See to dispense the Benedictine women from this "obligation," as he felt that their first priority in the New World was manual labor (assisting his monks, teaching, caring for orphans and hospitals). The women prayed for restoration of this privilege so important to them, and with the coming of the liturgical movement to the United States, their dream was realized. American Benedictine women invested personnel and energy into teaching chant—in Latin and in English—to their novices and professed members. In 1945–1946 the Divine Office was translated into English, and the Monastic Diurnal of 1948 had English on one side and Latin on the other side.

With Virgil Michel's death in 1938, Godfrey Diekmann (1909–2002), a confrere at Saint John's Abbey, assumed responsibility as editor of the magazine *Worship* and as director of the Liturgical Press. He was significantly involved in the Liturgical Weeks of the 1940s and 1950s that were begun and promoted by the Benedictines.

Diekmann was one of the consultants to the Pontifical Liturgical Preparatory Commission for the Second Vatican Council and was present for the final debates that resulted in the *Constitution on the Sacred Liturgy* (1963).

As with the Benedictine monasteries in Europe, American monasteries built extensive chant and liturgy collections to support the work of the monastery which is the Divine Office and to maintain the sources needed to transmit the chant tradition to succeeding generations. The Monastic Liturgy Forum and The Benedictine Musicians are two contemporary forums for sharing chant and liturgy resources. The Hill Museum and Manuscript Library at Saint John's University, Collegeville,

Minnesota, contains many original and microfiche copies of old manuscripts which are available for research.

With the Second Vatican Council

Chant thrives in the midst of healthy theological and liturgical development. Stagnancy kills the spirit of chant. As the church has become more conscious of the pastoral realities of a culturally diverse membership, liturgy has grown to embrace its many rites and expressions within those rites, enriching our experience of communal prayer.

The Divine Office had long consisted of multiple hours—Lauds, Prime, Terce, Sext, None, Vespers, Compline and Matins—but the church declared, with the *Constitution on the Sacred Liturgy*, that Lauds as morning prayer and Vespers as evening prayer were the hinges on which the Divine Office turns. While traditionally the entire book of Psalms was to be prayed each week, now the psalms may be distributed over longer periods of time.

Gregorian chant and sacred polyphony were preserved as the official prayer of the church. Praying the Divine Office in the vernacular was formally approved after the Second Vatican Council. The primacy of the Divine Office with its chant tradition was to continue. Benedictines continue to take this task seriously, as the primary work of monastic life.

Each monastery is free to create its own Office books, determining how many psalms are prayed each week, whether or not to retain Latin, and which translation of the vernacular to use, which modes to use, and so on. There is a universal character to the Divine Office at various monasteries, and yet each community expresses its individuality and something of the culture in how the Office is shaped.

In an address following a concert at the Sistine Chapel in June 2006, Pope Benedict XVI called for the continued preservation of the church's legacy of Gregorian chant and sacred polyphony, which he termed "a priceless spiritual, artistic, and cultural heritage."[12]

Conference of Benedictine Prioresses

> *Thus monks should practice this zeal with the warmest love: "Let them strive to be the first to honor one another." They should bear each other's weaknesses of both body and character with the utmost patience. They must compete with one another in obedience. No one should pursue what he judges advantageous to himself, but rather what benefits others. They must show selfless love to the brothers. Let them fear God out of love. They should love their abbot with sincere and humble charity. Let them prefer absolutely nothing to Christ, and may he lead us all together to everlasting life.* (RB 72:3-11)

The Conference of Benedictine Prioresses is an annual gathering of the leadership of women's Benedictine monasteries. Membership is voluntary and currently consists of houses from the Americas, Australia, and Ireland. Prioresses gather for mutual support, sharing of resources and wisdom, and continued growth.

Pope Pius XII supported the endeavors of women religious to improve their overall education and professional preparation. He also urged women religious to ponder the vision and charism of their founders with an eye to simplifying lifestyles and returning to the original vision. The Second Vatican Council reiterated this call. Benedictines took this mandate seriously and met together to study the Rule of Benedict and the monastic tradition in light of the demands of contemporary society.

Local, national, and international events as well as emerging spiritual needs have, on occasion, compelled the Conference of Benedictine Prioresses to address concerns in the form of written documents. With the call for renewal after the Second Vatican Council, the prioresses began writing documents originally intended for their own members. The process of creating these documents graced Benedictine women with the opportunity to prayerfully wrestle with important monastic subjects. Topics included were essential monastic values in *Upon This Tradition*, the Liturgy of the Hours in *Of Time Made Holy*, stewardship in *Of All Good Gifts*, the role of women in the church and society in *Toward Full Discipleship*, and the role of discernment in *With a Listening Heart*.

The prioresses have recognized another call to prayerfully ponder and respond in writing to this current moment in history as well. As Benedictines considered the contemporary monastic situation in light of the anniversary of the arrival of the first Benedictine women from Europe 150 years ago, prioresses sensed that there were striking similarities between contemporary challenges and those of the founding sisters. In light of the terrorist attacks in the United States and Europe, genocides in Rwanda, Kosovo, and Darfour, and ongoing wars in the Middle East, the prioresses felt called to put forward a different vision. At core was the concern that the present-day was now a culture of violence, a challenge frequently voiced by Pope John Paul II. The following excerpts from their document, *Wisdom from the Tradition: A Statement of North American Benedictine Women in Response to Our Times*, demonstrate how Benedictines define and live out concepts like obedience and authority in a way that is life-affirming and empowering, radically different from the way these terms are interpreted in the secular world.

Obedience: a Blessing to All

From a Culture of Domination to Life-Giving Authority

> Contemporary Western culture negates the value of obedience. It promotes, instead, individual decision-making and self-determination conducted in a vacuum of self-interest. Obedience in Western culture is associated with immaturity, lack of freedom, unpleasant restrictions and powerlessness. Obedience has sometimes been accused of making people dependent, weak and irresponsible. It is considered an essential feature of patriarchy. It is thought that obedience is required of people who are incapable of making informed, mature decisions, and adult women are counted among them.
>
> Unfortunately these charges about the meaning and effect of obedience have some merit, and the negation of obedience is one of the consequences of its distortions. Obedience has been used at times, both by the Church and political entities, as a weapon to keep people in positions of subjection and powerlessness, in the name of fidelity and piety or in the name of patriotism and loyalty. Even in our own communities we tell stories of injustices done among us because of this faulty equation of obedience with subjection.

Because of experiences of oppression and domination in the name of obedience, many people today find the concept of obedience to be distasteful and demeaning.

Fortunately, obedience that oppresses and victimizes is not the only model of obedience, as we ourselves have come to understand. Monastic obedience in the tradition of St. Benedict is based on respect for each person and her gifts. It does not demand conformity, uniformity, and childish blindness, but rather honors the diversity, individual conscience and personal dignity of the members. It is a distinctive approach to obedience because it is communal, consultative, relational, mutual and reasonable. Because of this it is life-giving. The purpose of monastic obedience, as envisioned by Benedict, is to enable the monastic to run to God with an expanded heart. Going one's own way makes the way to God more difficult.

Benedict's Vision of Obedience

Communal

Communion among the members of a monastery is at the heart of Benedictine obedience. The *Rule* prescribes a way of life in which people come together in order to go together to God. Many of the earliest monastics strove for union with God in solitude. An axiom in this way of spiritual life was "Stay in your cell; it will teach you everything." When these hermits attracted followers who wanted to learn the spiritual craft, they did not assemble their disciples into communities of sisters or brothers who might benefit not only from the wisdom of their chosen teacher but also from each other. Eremitical leaders who did establish a communal life sometimes did so for reasons of practicality more than principle. Few gave attention to the community itself as a means of spiritual development.

The monk Pachomius and subsequently Basil, Augustine and Benedict were among the first to recognize the value of the community in each individual's effort to seek God. Pachomius's very attraction to the Christian way of life rested in his experience of Christian community. Basil wondered how he could love his neighbors if he had no contact with them. Augustine pointed out the mutual responsibility of each member of the monastery for the progress of every other member. Benedict went a step further. He not only sought the salvation of individuals, but also prayed that Christ would bring all the members of the monastery *together* to everlasting life. In Benedict's vision the community itself, not just its members one by one, was on the way to God.

It is within this context of a community on its way to God that authority and obedience are exercised in a Benedictine monastery. Therefore, it is not simply a matter of a collection of individuals obeying a single superior. Rather, it is a matter of the total community seeking what is best for the spiritual welfare of each member and of the whole body. Monastics typically refer to this interdependence as a communal effort to discern the will of God. An individual chooses to obey because she trusts that what is being asked of her is in the best interest of the whole community with which she has cast her lot.

The interdependence of the individual good and the common good is an essential feature of Benedictine obedience. This is evident in the manner in which a novice makes profession. In his *Rule*, St. Benedict directs that she come before the whole community in the oratory and promise stability, fidelity to monastic life, and obedience (RB 58:17-18). While this is done in the presence of God and the saints, the promise is made to the community and the prioress. After making this promise, the novice prostrates herself before each member, asking for the prayer of her sisters. From that very day she is to be counted as one of the community (RB 58:23). The living out of her promise of obedience is supported by long-established monastic practices.

Consultative

In a Benedictine monastery, obedience is shown first of all to the prioress. Chosen by her sisters, the prioress is believed to hold the place of Christ in the community. This does not mean that she is free to exert her own will on the members, but that she, even more than the others, is responsible for discerning the will of God for the community. Benedict cautions against a prioress relying solely on her own abilities when trying to discover God's will in a particular circumstance. Rather, he advises her to solicit the advice of others.

The *Rule* provides for various methods of consultation. For the most important decisions, the prioress is to gather the whole community, explain the matter at hand and hear the advice of each member. For less important matters, the prioress is to seek the counsel of a few of the wiser and more experienced members of the community (RB 3).

An individual sister may also initiate consultation (RB 68). If she is assigned a task she finds burdensome or impossible to fulfill, she is encouraged to approach the prioress and explain her difficulty.

By including this provision in the *Rule*, Benedict acknowledges that the prioress must always be willing to listen before determining how to proceed.

Regardless of the manner in which the consultation is initiated, at the end of the discussion it is the prerogative of the prioress to determine what course of action is most prudent and for the community member to obey when the decision is made. However, the manner in which the consultation is conducted inevitably affects the outcome. For their part, the members of the monastery are to express their opinions with all humility, and not presume to defend their own views obstinately (RB 3:4-5). For her part, the prioress is to settle everything with foresight and fairness (RB 3:6). For this to happen, the relationships among community members must be solid.

Relational

Because obedience is meant to further the spiritual good of each one and all members of the monastery, it is necessarily relational. The primary model for relational obedience is the Holy Trinity. The three distinct Persons of the Trinity are so united in being and will that Christians call this mysterious unity "God," and affirm that "the source of love is [such a] God" (1 John 4).

In order to invite true obedience from her sisters, the prioress must know the individual members and their needs, strengths, weaknesses and deepest longings as clearly as possible. If the individual members are to offer advice regarding decisions that affect their sisters as much or even more than themselves, they too must know one another.

Relational obedience relies on trust. Each member must trust that the prioress and the other members have her best interests at heart so that she is willing to open herself to them. Secretiveness, suspicion or second-guessing of the motives of others breaks down trust in the monastery.

Relational obedience also relies on generosity of heart. Each sister must offer advice that is truly in the best interest of the others and the community as a whole, rather than cling stubbornly to whatever is to her own advantage. Rivalry, self-absorption, and excessive individualism are obstacles to the flourishing of authentic monastic obedience.

The trust that relational obedience requires can exist only where true charity prevails. Benedict describes this kind of charity as a good zeal which separates from evil and leads to God and everlasting life (RB 72:2). Among the signs of this charity, several are clearly named. The sisters show respect to each other; they support each other's weaknesses of body and behavior with the greatest patience, and each one pursues what is better for the others rather than what seems better for herself.

Mutual

Benedict expected that the members of the monastery obey not only the prioress but each other. Surprising to modern ears and sensibilities is Benedict's declaration that obedience is a blessing that is to be shown to all, since we know it is by this way of obedience that we go to God (RB 71:2). He envisioned the monastery as a place where the sisters earnestly compete in obedience to one another.

Mutual obedience is a way of ordering generous and healthy relationships among members of the community. Such obedience is a mature and adult response to—and even anticipation of—the needs of each other that brings about unity in the house of God. There is no place either for self-deprecating compliance or for efforts to prevail over others.

Reasonable

The accounts of the desert ascetics contain many stories of experienced hermits testing the obedience of newcomers. Perhaps the most quoted is that of the abba who ordered his disciple to persevere in watering a dead stick. The stories have a certain charm, but Benedict understood obedience differently. He did not ask his followers to undertake bizarre or useless tasks, but to perform ordinary and necessary tasks willingly and cheerfully.

Each member of the monastery is assigned useful work, which gives her a sense of belonging and of contributing to the common good. Benedict recognized that obedience does not exist as an end in itself, but for the good of the individual members and the community. Obedience in the spirit of the *Rule* is practical, purposeful and reasonable. It is heroic only in the sense that the sister must persevere in obeying day after day, month after month, year after year, for a lifetime.

Just as Christ was obedient unto death, Benedict realized that monastic obedience will require personal sacrifice. He promised not to establish anything unduly harsh or burdensome, but he admitted that the common good may at times call for a little strictness order to amend faults and to safeguard love (RB Prol 47).

When obedience is communal, consultative, relational, mutual and reasonable, it is indeed a blessing. Rather than fostering resentment, monastic obedience promotes good will. Rather than being exercised as tyranny, obedience wisely exercised opens the gates to personal freedom. It is not restrictive but expansive. It comes naturally to those who have come to cherish Christ and each other.

The Wisdom of Life-Giving Authority

Benedict understands that the purpose of authority is to author life. Authority is vested in the prioress, who is elected by the entire community. She exercises that authority for the benefit of the community as well as for the good of the individual members. For this reason the two goods must be balanced. Achieving that balance necessarily calls for open dialogue, prayerful listening and Spirit-filled discernment.

The Benedictine approach to making decisions sees each member of the group as having some share of the wisdom that is needed in order for the monastery to fulfill its purpose of seeking God and serving God's people. This requires that all voices are to be heard. Structures such as the monastic chapter and the monastic council[1] facilitate the process in which members offer their personal insights and listen to the insights of one another. The opinions and reflections of all enrich the process in the measure that they are all seeking God. The prioress, as facilitator of this communal discernment, strives to bring the group to a unified understanding. The purpose of the process is not to discover the majority view but rather to seek to know the will of God.

The prioress's role in the process goes beyond facilitation. She has genuine authority, and, having listened carefully to her sisters, she is finally responsible for setting the direction of community life and activity. As the *Rule* notes, she ponders the advice of all and follows what she judges to be the wiser course (RB 3:2). Since monastic authority is to be exercised to promote life, the prioress is accountable to all whose lives are touched by her decisions. In some instances, this may even include the monastery's neighbors and other related publics. Since the monastery is an ecclesial reality, the prioress is also accountable for the impact of community choices on the life of the local and universal Church. Ultimate monastic accountability, however, is to God, the One whom Benedictines seek together in steadfast love (RB 72).

The concept of authority according to the *Rule* presents an alternative to models of authority in which power can easily be misused for the self-aggrandizement of those who hold power. Authority exercised as the power to dominate is not life-giving but death-dealing. In a culture of domination, authority figures compete with one another, and their determination to prevail breeds conflict, corruption and violence. In this context, dissenting voices are suppressed without being listened to; the winner never admits mistakes, and the most powerful are accountable to no one.

In contrast, wise Benedictine authority seeks to foster peace in the community in order that all members can truly seek God. The exercise of authority aspires to facilitate, to empower and to promote the well-being of the community. In this environment, individuals are regularly called forth to serve the community and the community's publics in ways they might never have imagined. The prioress, having herself been called to service in the community, will call on other sisters to use talents and abilities that they themselves might fail to recognize. As individual gifts are released and shared, the entire community is enriched.

Benedict organizes the monastic community as a human setting in which people accompany one another through life. By their monastic profession the sisters take responsibility with and for one another. They encourage and assist each other, "supporting with the greatest patience one another's weaknesses of body or behavior" (RB 72:5). In order for this vision to flourish, there must be order and harmony, and creating and preserving this order is one of the functions of authority. St. Benedict knew from experience that when the members are distressed and disquieted they do not give their wholehearted attention to their monastic call to seek God.

The Blessings of Obedience

Individual

What blessings can an individual monastic find in obedience? The Benedictine woman has come to community to truly seek God and thereby to find abundance of life. Her seeking of God is done in the context of community; for it is there that the sister aspires to find happiness in following the will of God. Her ongoing challenge is always to discern what God desires of her within her community.

She may begin by searching her own heart and prayerfully pondering the Word of God in the biblical Word. But these solitary efforts are limited and insufficient, and they may leave the way to God clouded, confused, and obscured by her lack of understanding or her conscious or unconscious self-interest. Obedience is the gift that aids her in finding her way forward.

Benedictine obedience involves the work of listening attentively to the community and to the prioress, who holds the place of Christ. Through honest, sincere, and open dialogue with the prioress and her sisters, the way becomes clearer, self-interest is recognized and the common good is clarified. The sister finds peace in this process, trusting that God will be with her as she listens and responds. With faith, she walks confidently on the path to salvation even when it seems straight and narrow.

The purpose of Benedictine obedience is not to limit, suppress, or crush the will of the individual as if it were malfunctioning or evil. The purpose is to guide the sister toward the fullness of life. It often happens that a sister's assessment of her gifts, talents and abilities is distorted by family history, past experiences and the circumstances of her life. Others can often see talents and hopes in her that lie buried beneath fear, apprehension, diminished self-worth or caution. Obedience calls her to stretch her expectations of herself and to move beyond self-imposed limitations. Monastic obedience, while appearing to require total negation of the self, actually leads a person to an existential freedom. Obedience calls forth gifts that were lying dormant and brings into existence previously untested skills. Inherent capabilities are drawn forth and unsuspected potential is realized. Many sisters can recall receiving appointments that challenged them to develop gifts they never knew they possessed. The benefits of obedience in community await expression for the monastic who risks it.

It may seem simpler and quicker for a sister to make her own decisions independently of the prioress and community. But then there is limited wisdom and experience to inform the decision-making process. Through obedience the sister has access to the wisdom of others who bear the richness of varied experience and education. In the practice of obedience, a sister stands with her prioress and community as a seeker of God. She trusts that they are on the same search and that they are aware of her personal gifts and weaknesses and can recognize her capabilities. As difficult as this readiness to listen may be, it is a prerequisite for the encouragement of unselfish interpersonal relationships among members. The call to assist one another in discernment is an important element on the Benedictine monastic path to union with God.

Communal

Obedience brings blessings to the community as well as to its individual members. A community comprised of mutual listeners is a community hospitable to peace and charity. Harmony breathes where people truly listen, respect and respond to one another. The Holy Spirit is set free in this kind of community.

When each member is open and responsive to the guidance and wisdom of the prioress and community, she participates in a mission larger than herself. Because of the willingness of members to move beyond their own vision, the community can make long-term commitments to ministries and sisters can join with one another in corporate ministries that none of them could accomplish alone.

Where all are guided by a common vision, the common energy creates a powerful force for the service of the Gospel. Historically, the obedience of sisters to the needs of the Church and their communities was largely responsible for the success of the Catholic school system and the Catholic health care system in North America. Obedience continues to empower and enable our communities of ecclesial women to make commitments to ministries needed today, among them works for justice and peace, spiritual formation and spiritual care, and promotion of the well-being of women.

Conclusion

Our relationship within our societies and our interactions with the planet and its atmosphere are distorted by our lack of mutuality and interdependence. Although we live in a time where the way of self-aggrandizement has spawned cultural responses of fear and struggles for domination, our vocation as Benedictine women has graced us to see that the practice of mutual respect and obedience is a vital force for human well-being.[2]

Afterword

Pope Pius XI (1857–1939) referred to the Benedictine world as "an Order without order." Despite "reforming" efforts that have sometimes been more "conforming" efforts, the Benedictine heart is fiercely autonomous and will buck against efforts at conforming. However, we thrive in being connected with others: other monastics, the local community, and the global community.

Every Benedictine monastery is autonomous. Most belong to a Federation, Congregation, or Confederation—each essentially the same kind of structure by differing names. These are monasteries gathered or grouped according to historic foundation or because of particular shared vision. The affiliation allows monasteries to learn from one another and hold each other accountable for the monastic observances. New foundations, often called priories, are connected to their founding house until independence is achieved. What ultimately binds Benedictines together is the gospel, the Rule of Benedict, the monastic tradition, and fifteen hundred years of lived experience.

Since 1893 there has been an office of the Abbot Primate in Rome, which serves as an informal gathering place for Benedictine men, operates a pontifical university, and hosts international gatherings of men. The Abbot Primate's relationship with the men is spiritual; he and his office do not replace any abbot. The Abbot Primate also connects with the Holy See on behalf of Benedictine men, and informally on behalf of Benedictine women. Benedictine women connect globally through the *Communio Internationalis Benedictarum.*

The Cistercians and the Trappists also have representation to the Vatican. Offices in Rome were established for the Abbot Generals of each tradition. Now connected to the internet, there are helpful websites, including www.osb-international.info/index/en.html, www.osb.org, www.ocist.org, and www.ocso.org.

Current statistics indicate that there are approximately ten thousand monks among the major expressions of monastic life (Benedictine, Cistercian, Trappist, and Camaldolese). For monastic women, there are approximately eighteen thousand nuns and sisters.

In our contemporary world, there are Benedictine houses in the Anglican/Episcopalian, Methodist, and Lutheran traditions, and increasingly ecumenical monasteries. Ecumenical monasteries, in the tradition of Taizé, welcome Christians of any expression into the monastery. Usually members attend Sunday services of their choice with the common prayer of the monastery being the Liturgy of the Hours. These monastics usually connect with other monastics in their region while not formally connecting with the Holy See.

Benedictines do not have a standard ministry. Benedictines share a common life, pray the Divine Office, and work to support the community with something left over for the poor. As much as possible, monasteries are self-supporting. A person does not enter a monastery for a mission, as do many candidates at other religious orders, rather a person enters a monastery to seek God. Yet Benedictines do not seek God only in silence and prayer. Their motto *ora et labora* means "prayer and work," which are balanced in the Benedictine life. Monasteries are connected to the local church and prevailing culture, and the needs of the local people have a significant impact on monastic decisions. Benedictines have taught farming techniques; mediated talks in the midst of political strife; opened and operated schools and orphanages; provided spiritual formation to those called to spiritual direction; established and supported food banks and shelters and provided services for the homeless; cared for the elderly; and worked for peace. Most monasteries have histories of changing ministries as the prevailing needs of the region shifted.

Although they share a core spirituality and life according to the Rule, each Benedictine monastery has a unique character or personality, reflecting the culture or cultures within its house and the local area. Each monastery continually discerns God's call in their lives. Benedictines, as all who follow the Gospel, are called to be in the world but not of the world. Benedictines must continually challenge themselves to promote what is good and reject what is harmful about a given culture. Benedictines are called to be prophetic, both in their own lives and in the world around them.

Benedictines continue to struggle, in the very best sense of the word, with following God's will. Our historical memory reminds us that what is today has been in the past and will be yet again in the future. God is with us.

While membership in monasteries appears to be dwindling in most parts of the world, interest in Benedictine spirituality is not waning. Oblates are people who value the Benedictine way of life, finding personal meaning in the Rule of Benedict and Benedictine spirituality. They associate themselves with a particular monastery and make an oblation (an offering of themselves) to the Benedictine way of life while continuing to live with their families and hold jobs. Oblates are secular Benedictines who seek to bring Benedictine spirituality to broader society. Oblates oftentimes gather together at their monasteries, and at national and international oblate gatherings. They publish on Benedictine spirituality as well as in other areas of theology, and are a significant gift to the future of Benedictine life. As in the houses themselves, Benedictine Oblates come from many different Christian traditions, including Anglican/Episcopalian, Methodist, and Lutheran. Oblate communities are very ecumenical, again drawn by the prayer life and the values of Benedict's Rule.

Benedictines are involved in ecumenism and interfaith dialogue. At the formal level, Benedictines are actively involved in dialogue with Buddhists and Hindu monastics, both encouraging one another as well as in challenging each other to be true to the monastic tradition and call. Increasingly Benedictines are establishing Christian ashrams and ecumenical monasteries, meeting with monastics of the Orthodox tradition, and gathering regularly in formal dialogues, often organized through Monastic Interreligious Dialogue.

New monasteries are being founded literally all over the world. Some are ecumenical Benedictine communities; some are mixed communities of Benedictines where families with children, singles, and vowed celibates share the common life. Monasteries are also connecting with each other outside formal structures to share resources and educational opportunities; the Alliance for International Monasticism has been one vehicle for connecting communities across cultures and political divides.

As with many expressions of religious life, the future is uncertain for Benedictines. However, Benedictines have lived through closures of monasteries (either due to political unrest or dwindling membership) and "vocation crises" in the past fifteen centuries. What Benedictines are confident of is that there will indeed be a future.

Selections from the Rule of Benedict

PROLOGUE

1. Listen, O my son, to the teachings of your master, and turn to them with the ear of your heart. Willingly accept the advice of a devoted father and put it into action. 2. Thus you will return by the labor of obedience to the one from whom you drifted through the inertia of disobedience. 3. Now then I address my words to you: whoever is willing to renounce self will, and take up the powerful and shining weapons of obedience to fight for the Lord Christ, the true king.

4. First, when you set out to do some good work, beg him with most insistent prayer to bring it to completion. 5. Then the one who has already been so good as to count us among the number of his sons may never have to rage over our evil actions. 6. By means of the good things he has given us, we should at all times obey him so that he will not disinherit us like an angry father does his sons. 7. Nor will he, like a fearsome lord enraged by our offenses, give us over to perpetual punishment as wicked slaves who did not wish to follow him to glory.

8. Therefore, let us rise at long last, for Scripture stirs us with the words: "It is high time we rose from sleep" (Rom 13:11). 9. Let us open our eyes to the divine light, and let us listen with astonished ears to the warning of the divine voice, which daily cries out to us: 10. "Today, if you hear his voice, do not harden your hearts" (Ps 94:8). 11. And again: "Whoever has ears for hearing should listen to what the Spirit says to the churches" (Rev 2:7). 12. And what does the Spirit say? "Come, children, hear me; I will teach you the fear of the Lord" (Ps 34:12). 13. "Run while you have the light of life, that the darkness not overtake you" (John 12:35).

14. The Lord, seeking a worker for himself in the crowds to whom he cries out, says: 15. "Which of you desires life and longs to see good

days?" (Ps 34:13). 16. If you hear this and respond "I do!" God says to you: 17. "If you desire true and lasting life, keep your tongue from evil and your lips from speaking deceit; avoid evil and do good, seek peace and pursue it. 18. When you have done this, my eyes will be on you and my ears will attend to your prayers; before you even invoke me, I will say: 'Here I am!'" (Ps 34:14-16; Isa 58:9; 65:24). 19. What could be sweeter, dearest brothers, than this voice of the Lord, who invites us? 20. Look, the Lord in his devotion to us shows us the way to life. 21. Therefore, let us belt our waist with faith that leads to the performance of good works. Let us set out on his path with the Gospel as our guide so that we may be worthy to see him who called us into his kingdom.

22. If we wish to dwell in the tent of his kingdom we shall not arrive unless we run there by good deeds. 23. But let us ask the Lord with the Prophet, saying: "Lord, who will dwell in your tent, or who will rest on your holy mountain?" (Ps 15:1). 24. After this question, brothers, listen to the Lord's response, which shows us the way to his tent: 25. "The person who walks blamelessly and acts justly" (Ps 15:2); 26. who speaks the truth candidly and has not committed fraud with his tongue (Ps 15:3); 27. who does the neighbors no ill, nor listens to slander against him" (Ps 15:3). 28. When the wicked one, the devil, suggests something, he pushes both him and his advice out of the sight of his heart; he annihilates (the satanic) incipient thoughts, taking them and smashing them against Christ. 29. The fear of the Lord keeps these people from vaunting themselves for their good performance, for they know that what is good in themselves could not have come about except for the Lord. 30. They heap praise on the Lord working in them, saying with the prophet: "Not to us, Lord, not to us, but to your name give the glory" (Ps 115:1). 31. Likewise, the Apostle Paul took no credit for his preaching, simply saying: "I am what I am due to God's grace" (1 Cor 15:10). 32. And again, he says: "Whoever boasts should boast in the Lord" (2 Cor 10:17). 33. Thus the Lord says in the Gospel: "Whoever hears my words and does them I liken to the prudent person who built a house on a rock. The floods came, the winds blew and battered that house, but it did not collapse because it was founded on rock" (Matt 7:24-25).

35. Having finished his discourse, the Lord waits for us to respond by action every day to his holy warnings. 36. Therefore the days of this life are given us as a time of truce for the correction of our faults. 37. The Apostle says: "Don't you know that the patience of God leads you to repentance?" (Rom 2:4). 38. For the Lord in his benevolence says: "I do not wish the death of the sinner, but rather that he change his ways and live" (Ezek 33:11). 39. And so, brothers, we have queried the Lord about

what is required of a dweller in his tent, and we have received the teaching about dwelling there. The question is—will we fulfil the duties of an inhabitant? 40. Therefore we must prepare our hearts and our bodies to wage the battle of holy obedience to his precepts. 41. Let us pray the Lord to command the help of his grace to aid us in that which we cannot accomplish by nature. 42. And if we wish to flee the punishment of hell and attain eternal life, 43. while there is still time and we are still in this body, and there remains time to accomplish all this in the light of this life, 44. we must run and accomplish now what will profit us for eternity.

45. Therefore we must establish a school for the Lord's service. 46. In its organization, we have tried not to create anything grim or oppressive. 47. In a given case we may have to arrange things a bit strictly to correct vice or preserve charity. 48. When that happens, do not immediately take fright and flee the path of salvation, which can only be narrow at its outset. 49. But as we progress in the monastic life and in faith, our hearts will swell with the unspeakable sweetness of love, enabling us to race along the way of God's commandments. 50. Then we will never depart from his teaching and we will persevere in his doctrine in the monastery until death. Likewise, we will participate in the passion of Christ through patience so as to deserve to be companions in his kingdom. Amen.

Benedictine Values: Chapters 4–7

RB 4: WHAT ARE THE TOOLS OF GOOD WORKS?

1. First, to love the Lord God with all your heart, all your soul and all your strength, 2. then, your neighbor as yourself, 3. then, not to kill, 4. not to commit adultery, 5. not to steal, 6. not to covet, 7. not to give false witness, 8. to honor all persons 9. and not to do to another what you do not want done to yourself.

10. Deny yourself in order to follow Christ. 11. Chastise the body. 12. Do not cling to pleasures. 13. Love fasting. 14. Assist the poor. 15. Clothe the naked. 16. Visit the sick. 17. Bury the dead. 18. Come to the aid of those in trouble. 19. Console the sorrowful.

20. You should become a stranger to the world's ways. 21. Prefer nothing to the love of Christ. 22. Do not act under the impulse of anger. 23. Do not wait for vengeance. 24. Do not plot deceit. 25. Do not give a false peace. 26. Do not abandon charity. 27. Do not swear oaths for fear of swearing falsely. 28. Speak the truth both in your heart and with your mouth.

29. Do not return evil for evil. 30. Do not wrong others, but suffer patiently the wrongs done to you. 31. Love your enemies. 32. Do not curse those who curse you, but bless them instead. 33. Bear persecution on behalf of justice.

34. Do not be proud, 35. nor a great wine-drinker. 36. Do not be a glutton, 37. nor indulge in excessive sleep. 38. Do not be a loafer, 39. nor a grumbler, 40. nor one who runs down the reputation of others.

41. Put your hope in God. 42. When you see something good in yourself, credit it to God, not to yourself. 43. As for evil, know that you are always the agent of it, and therefore take responsibility.

44. Fear Judgment Day. 45. Have a healthy fear of hell. 46. Long for eternal life with the desire of the Spirit. 47. Keep your eye on death every day. 48. Maintain a strict control over your actions at every moment. 49. Know for sure that God sees you wherever you are. 50. When bad thoughts arrive in your heart, smash them against Christ and manifest them to a spiritual elder. 51. Close your mouth on evil and perverse talk. 52. Do not get in the habit of long-winded conversations. 53. Do not engage in empty babbling or joking. 54. Don't indulge in prolonged or explosive laughter.

55. Listen intently to holy readings. 56. Give yourself frequently to prayer. 57. Confess your past sins to God with tears and groaning at daily prayer. 58. Correct these sins for the future.

59. Do not carry out the urgings of the flesh. 60. Hate your own will. 61. Obey the abbot's orders in all things, even if he—God forbid—acts otherwise. Remember the Lord's command: Do what they say, not what they do.

62. Do not wish to be called holy before you really are; first be holy, and then the term will be truer in your case. 63. You must put the commands of God into action every day. 64. Love chastity. 65. Hate no one. 66. Do not be jealous. 67. Do not act out of envy. 68. Do not be habitually quarrelsome. 69. Flee pride. 70. Respect the seniors. 71. Love the juniors. 72. Pray for your enemies for the love of Christ. 73. If you have a quarrel with someone, make peace before sundown. 74. And never despair of God's mercy.

75. These, then, are the tools of the spiritual craft. 76. If we have wielded them ceaselessly day and night, and returned them on Judgment Day, we will receive that reward from the Lord which he promised: 77. What eye has not seen nor ear heard, God has prepared for those who love him. 78. The workshop where we should work hard at all these things is the monastic enclosure and stability in the community.

RB 5: OBEDIENCE

1. The basic road to progress for the humble person is through prompt obedience. 2. This is characteristic of those who hold Christ more precious than all else. 3. For that reason, on account of the holy service they have professed, and because of the fear of hell and the glory of eternal life, 4. as soon as something is commanded by the superior, they waste no time in executing it as if it were divinely commanded. 5. The Lord says of them: "When he heard me, he obeyed me." 6. Likewise, he says to teachers: "Whoever listens to you listens to me." Therefore, such people immediately abandon their own affairs and put aside self-will. 8. They immediately empty their hands, dropping whatever they are doing to carry out with the quick step of obedience the order of the one who commands. 9. It is as if the order were given by the master and carried out by the disciple at the same instant. Both command and response take place almost simultaneously with an alacrity caused by the fear of the Lord. 10. It is love that drives these people to progress toward eternal life.

11. Therefore they seize on the narrow way, of which the Lord says: "The route that leads to life is narrow." 12. That is why they do not wish to live by their own lights, obeying their own desires and wants. Rather, they prefer to walk according to the judgment and command of another, living in cenobitic community with an abbot over them. 13. Doubtless, people such as these imitate the Lord, who said: "I did not come to do my own will, but the will of the one who sent me."

14. But this same obedience will only be acceptable to God and humanly attractive if the command is not executed fearfully, slowly or listlessly, nor with murmuring or refusal. 15. For obedience given to superiors is given to God, who said: "Whoever listens to you, listens to me." 16. And it should be given gladly by disciples, for "God loves a cheerful giver." 17. If a disciple obeys grudgingly and murmurs not only out loud but internally, 18. even if he carries out the order, it will not be acceptable to God. For he sees the heart of the murmurer, 19. who will receive no thanks for such a deed. On the contrary if he does not make satisfaction, he will receive the penalty of murmurers.

RB 6: ON SILENCE

1. Let us do what the Prophet says: "I said: 'I will guard my ways so as not to sin with my tongue. I placed a guard at my mouth. I was

speechless and humiliated, refraining even from good speech.'" 2. Here the Prophet shows that if we sometimes ought to refrain from speaking good words on account of the intrinsic value of silence, so much the more ought we stop speaking evil words out of fear that it will be punished as sin. 3. Therefore, due to the great importance of silence itself, perfect disciples should rarely be granted permission to speak, even good, holy and edifying words. 4. For it is written: "In much speaking, you will not avoid sin." 5. And elsewhere, "Death and life are in the hands of the tongue." 6. It is the master's role to speak and teach; the disciple is to keep silent and listen. 7. Therefore, if one must ask something from the superior, let it be done with great humility and reverent submission. 8. As for crude jokes and idle talk aimed at arousing laughter, we put an absolute clamp on them in all places. We do not permit the disciple to so much as open his mouth for such talk.

RB 7: ON HUMILITY

1. Brothers, the Holy Scripture cries out to us, saying: *Whoever is self-promoting will be humbled, and whoever is humble will be promoted.* 2. When it says this, it shows us that all self-promotion is a kind of pride. 3. The Prophet shows that he avoids this when he says: *Lord, my heart is not lifted up, nor are my eyes fixed on the heights. I have not mixed myself in great affairs nor in things too wonderful for me.* 4. But what *if my thoughts are not humble? What if I rise up in pride? Then you will refuse me like a mother does a weaned child.*

5. So, brothers, if we wish to arrive at the pinnacle of humility and if we wish to attain speedily to the heavenly height to which one climbs by humility in this present life, 6. then by our ascending acts we must set up that ladder which appeared to Jacob in a dream. It showed him *angels descending and ascending*. 7. Doubtless, we should understand this descent and ascent as follows: one descends by pride and ascends by humility. 8. The towering ladder is, of course, our earthly life. When the heart is humble, God raises it up to heaven. 9. We could say that our body and soul are the sides of this ladder, into which the divine summons has inserted various rungs of humility and discipline for the ascent.

10. Thus the first step of humility is to utterly flee forgetfulness by keeping the fear of God always before one's eyes. 11. We must constantly recall the commandments of God, continually mulling over how hell burns the sinners who despise God, and eternal life is prepared for those who fear God. 12. We should guard ourselves at all times from sins and

vices, that is, of thoughts, tongue, hands, feet or self-will, but also desires of the flesh.

13. Let each one take into account that he is constantly observed by God from heaven and our deeds everywhere lie open to the divine gaze and are reported by the angels at every hour. 14. The Prophet demonstrates this to us when he shows that God is always privy to our thoughts: *God examines hearts and minds.* 15. Likewise, *The Lord knows human thoughts.* 16. And again, *You have known my thoughts from afar.* 17. Human thoughts will be made plain to you. 18. So, then, to be careful about his bad thoughts, the faithful brother should say in his heart: *I will be blameless before him if I restrain myself from my evil.*

19. As for self-will, we are forbidden to carry it out, for Scripture says to us: *Beware of your own desires.* And so we ask God in prayer that his will be accomplished in us. 21. Thus it is with good reason that we learn to steer clear of our own will, for we dread the warning of Holy Scripture: *There are paths that seem straight to us, but ultimately they plunge into the depths of hell.* 22. We also find frightening what is said to the careless: *They are decadent and have become abominable through following their desires.*

23. We should be convinced that our lower inclinations are well known to God, for the Prophet says to God: *All my desire is before you.* 24. Thus it is imperative that we beware of evil desire, for death lurks near the gateway of pleasure. 25. That is why Scripture commands: *Do not pursue your lusts.*

26. Therefore, if *the eyes of the Lord survey the good and the bad,* 27. and *the Lord constantly looks down from heaven on the human race to see if there is anyone with the wisdom to seek God,* 28. and if the angels assigned to us report our deeds to the Lord daily, even day and night, 29. then, brothers, we must continually make sure, as the psalmist says, that God never sees us *falling* into evil and becoming *useless people.* 30. Because he is merciful, he may spare us now and hope we change for the better, but eventually he will say, *You did these things and I was silent.*

31. The second step of humility is not to delight in satisfying our desires out of love for our own way. 32. Rather, we should pattern our behavior on that saying of the Lord: *I have not come to do my own will but the will of him who sent me.* 33. Scripture also says: *Self-will brings punishment [on itself] but obedience to duty merits a reward.*

34. The third step of humility is to submit to the superior in all obedience for love of God. In this, we imitate the Lord, of whom the Apostle says: *He became obedient to the point of death.*

35. The fourth step of humility is this: when obedience involves harsh, hostile things or even injustice of some sort, one embraces them patiently with no outcry. 36. Let us bear such things without flagging or fleeing, as Scripture says: *Whoever perseveres to the end will be saved.* 37. Likewise, *Let your heart be strengthened and endure the trials of the Lord.* 38. To show that the faithful person ought to endure all adversities for the Lord's sake, the Prophet says on behalf of the suffering: *All day long we are put to death on your account; we are considered as sheep for the slaughter.* 39. But they are so hopeful of divine vindication that they joyfully stay their course, saying: *In all these things we triumph because of him who loved us.* 40. And in another place Scripture says something similar: *You have tried us, O God; you have tested us with fire, as silver is tested. You have led us into a trap. You have loaded our backs with trouble.* 41. And to show that we ought to be under a superior, it goes on to say: *You have placed people over our heads.* 42. Moreover, those who maintain patience in the face of setbacks and injustices fulfill the command of the Lord: *When they are slapped on the cheek, they present the other one as well. When someone takes their shirt, they give up their coat as well. Pressed into service for one mile, they go two.* 43. Like the Apostle Paul, they endure with *disloyal brothers and persecution; they bless those who curse them.*

44. The fifth step consists in revealing through humble confession to one's abbot all evil thoughts that enter the heart, as well as the evils secretly committed. 45. Scripture urges us on in this matter when it says: *Make plain your way to the Lord, and hope in him.* 46. It also says: *Confess to the Lord, for he is good. His mercy is forever.* 47. The Prophet says further: *I have made my sin known to you and not hidden my injustices.* 48. I said: *I will accuse myself to the Lord of my injustices. And you forgave the sin of my heart.*

49. The sixth step occurs when a monk is content with low and dishonorable treatment. And regarding all that is commanded him, he thinks of himself as a bad and worthless worker, 50. saying with the Prophet: *I was reduced to impotence and ignorance; I was like a brute beast before you, and I am also with you.*

51. The seventh step of humility is surmounted if the monk not only confesses with his tongue, but also believes with all his heart that he is lower and less honorable than all the rest. 52. He thus abases himself, declaring with the Prophet: *I, though, am a worm, not a man. I am the object of curses and rejection.* 53. *I was raised up, but now I am humiliated and covered with confusion.* 54. Along the same line: *It is good for me that you humiliate me, so that I might learn your commandments.*

55. The eighth step of humility is when a monk does nothing except what is encouraged by the common rule of the monastery and the example of the veteran members of the community.

56. The ninth step of humility comes when a monk holds back his tongue from speaking, and out of love for silence does not speak until someone asks him a question. 57. Scripture shows that *In much talk, one does not escape sin*, 58. and: *The chatterbox does not walk straight on the earth.*

59. The tenth step of humility consists in not being quick to laugh at the slightest provocation, for it is written: *The fool raises his voice in laughter*.

60. The eleventh step of humility is that when a monk speaks at all, he does so gently and without laughter, humbly and seriously, with few and careful words. 61. And let him not be given to shouting, as it stands written: *The wise man is known by his reticence*.

62. The twelfth step of humility is achieved when a monk's humility is not only in his heart, but is apparent in his very body to those who see him. 63. That is, whether he is at the Work of God, in the oratory, in the monastery, in the garden, on a journey, in the field or anywhere at all, whether sitting, walking or standing, let his head always be bowed and his gaze be fixed on the earth. 64. Constantly aware of his guilt for sins, he should consider himself to be already standing before the terrifying judgment of God. 65. He should always repeat in his heart what the publican said in the gospel, his eyes cast downward: *Lord, I am a sinner and not worthy to raise my eyes to heaven*. 66. And also with the Prophet: *I am bowed down and totally humbled*.

67. Therefore, when he has climbed all these steps of humility, the monk will soon arrive at that *perfect love of God which drives out fear*. 68. Due to this love, he can now begin to accomplish effortlessly, as if spontaneously, everything that he previously did out of fear. 69. He will do this no longer out of fear of hell but out of love for Christ, good habit itself and a delight in virtue. 70. Once his worker has been cleansed of vices and sins, the Lord will graciously make all this shine forth in him by the power of the Holy Spirit.

The Divine Office: Chapters 8–10

RB 8: THE DIVINE OFFICE AT NIGHT

1. In wintertime, that is, from November first until Easter, right reason dictates they should arise at the eighth hour of the night. 2. That way they can rest a little more than half the night and rise with their food

digested. 3. The time that remains after Vigils should be used for the learning of psalms and lessons by those brothers who need to do so.

4. From Easter to the aforesaid November first, the time is to be regulated as follows: Vigils should be followed immediately by Matins at daybreak, with a very short interval in between, when the brothers can go out for the demands of nature.

RB 9: HOW MANY PSALMS SHOULD BE SUNG AT THE NIGHT OFFICE?

1. In the previously defined winter season, first this verse is repeated three times: "Lord, open my lips, and my mouth will proclaim your praise." 2. To this should be added Psalm 3 and the Gloria. 3. After this comes Psalm 94 with refrain, or at least sung. 4. The Ambrosian hymn follows, and six psalms with antiphons.

5. When these have been completed, the verse is sung, the abbot gives his blessing and all the monks sit down on the benches. Then the brothers should read in turn three lessons from the book on the lectern. Three responses should be sung in between the lessons. 6. Two responses should be said without Gloria, but after the third, the singer chants the Gloria. 7. When the chanter begins the Gloria, all must immediately rise from their seats out of respect and reverence for the Holy Trinity. 8. The books read at Vigils should have divine authority, whether from the Old or New Testament. The biblical commentaries of renowned and Orthodox Catholic Fathers may also be used.

9. After these three lessons with their responses, the six remaining psalms follow, to be sung with Alleluia. 10. The lesson of the Apostle follows these, and it is done by heart. Then comes the verse and litany of petition, which is Kyrie Eleison. 11. Thus ends the nocturnal Vigils.

RB 10: HOW THE NIGHT OFFICE SHOULD BE DONE IN SUMMERTIME

1. From Easter to November first, however, the number of psalms is maintained as stated above. 2. But the lessons in the book are not to be read, owing to the shortness of the nights. In place of three lessons, one Old Testament lesson is said by heart, and a brief response is added to it. 3. All the rest is performed as prescribed, that is, never fewer than the equivalent of twelve psalms must be sung at Night Vigils, not counting Psalms 3 and 94.

Life in the Monastery: Chapters 33–40

RB 33: WHETHER THE MONKS SHOULD CONSIDER ANYTHING THEIR OWN

1. This vice in particular must be torn up by the roots: 2. that anyone should presume to give or receive anything without the abbot's permission, 3. or consider anything personal property, absolutely nothing: no book, no writing tablets, no stylus—nothing whatsoever. 4. That is because they have neither their bodies nor their own wills at their own disposal. 5. Rather, they should ask for all they need from the father of the monastery. And it is not permissible to have anything that the abbot does not give or permit. 6. *Let all things be common to all*, as Scripture says, *so that no one may* presume *to call* anything his own. 7. But if anyone is caught indulging in this most detestable vice, let him be warned once and a second time. 8. If there is no improvement, he should be punished.

RB 34: WHETHER ALL SHOULD RECEIVE NECESSITIES IN EQUAL MEASURE

1. As it is written: *It was distributed to each one according to need*. 2. By this we do not recommend favoritism—God forbid!—but sympathy for weaknesses. 3. So the one who needs less should thank God and not be sad. 4. And whoever needs more should be humble about his weaknesses and not gloat over the mercy shown him. 5. Thus all the members will be at peace. 6. Above all, the evil of murmuring must not appear for any cause by any word or gesture whatsoever. 7. If anyone is caught doing this, he should undergo a rather severe punishment.

RB 35: THE WEEKLY KITCHEN SERVERS

1. The brothers should serve one another. Therefore no one may be excused from kitchen duty except for illness or occupation with an essential task, 2. for thus is merit increased and love built up. 3. Let help be provided for the weak so they do not lose heart in this work, 4. but let all have help according to the size of the community or the circumstances of the place. 5. If the community is rather large, the cellarer should be excused from the kitchen. As we have said, those occupied with essential tasks should also be excused. 6. The others should serve one another in love.

7. One who is about to complete the week's work should do the cleaning on Saturday. 8. They should wash the towels the brothers use to dry their hands and feet. 9. Moreover, both the one completing service and the one beginning it should wash the feet of all. 10. He should return the utensils of his service to the cellarer clean and intact. 11. The cellarer should, in his turn, give them to the one entering the week, noting what he gives out and what he receives back.

12. One hour before mealtime, the weekly servers should each receive a drink and a piece of bread over and above the standard portion. 13. Then they can serve the brethren at mealtime without grumbling and undue fatigue. 14. On solemn feast days, however, they should wait till the final meal prayer.

15. As soon as Sunday Lauds is finished, both the beginning and the finishing weekly servers should bow before the knees of all in the oratory, begging for prayers. 16. The one finishing the week should say this verse: *Blessed are you, Lord God, for you have aided me and comforted me.* 17. When this has been repeated three times and the departing server has received the blessing, the one entering upon service should say: *God, come to my assistance; Lord, hasten to help me.* 18. This verse too should be repeated three times by all. He should be blessed and let him then begin his week of service.

RB 36: THE SICK BROTHERS

1. The sick are to be cared for before and above all else, for it is really Christ who is served in them. 2. He himself said: *I was sick and you visited me,* and 3. *Whatever you did to one of these little ones, you did to me.* 4. For their part, the sick should keep in mind that they are being served out of respect for God. Therefore they should not irritate the brothers serving them with excessive demands. 5. Nonetheless, they should be treated with patience, for in doing so one merits a generous reward. 6. So the abbot must be very careful that they suffer no neglect whatever.

7. The sick brothers should be provided with a separate room and a server who is God-fearing, devoted and careful. 8. The sick should be granted the use of baths as often as it seems useful, but they should be allowed less readily to the healthy, and especially to the young. 9. The eating of meat should be allowed to the very weak to build up their strength. When they have recuperated, however, all must abstain from meat in the accustomed manner.

10. The abbot should be extremely careful that the sick not be neglected either by the cellarers or the servers. He is responsible for whatever faults the disciples commit.

RB 37: THE AGED AND CHILDREN

1. While human nature itself is indulgent toward these two groups, namely the aged and children, the authority of the Rule should also look out for them. 2. Their weakness must always be kept in mind and the strictness of the Rule regarding food should not be imposed on them. 3. Rather, let them be treated with loving consideration: they should (eat) before the regular time.

RB 38: THE WEEKLY READER

1. The meals of the brothers ought not to lack reading, nor should just anyone who happens to pick up the book read there. Rather, the one who is to read should begin on Sunday and do so for the whole week. 2. After Mass and Communion, the one beginning the week should petition all to pray for him, that God might protect him from the spirit of pride. 3. And let all recite this verse three times in the oratory, with the reader beginning it: *Lord, open my lips, and my mouth will proclaim your praise.* 4. When he has received the blessing, let him begin the week of reading.

5. Profound silence should reign there, so that the only voice heard will be that of the reader and not of anyone else whispering or talking. 6. As they eat and drink, the brothers should serve the needs of one another so that no one need ask for anything. 7. If it is necessary, however, one should make his request by some audible signal rather than by voice. 8. No one should presume to ask questions about the reading or about anything else, *in case the devil be given an opening*. 9. The superior may wish, though, to make a brief remark for edification.

10. The brother who is the weekly reader should receive some doctored wine before he reads. This is because of the Holy Communion and because he may find it difficult to endure the fast. 11. He should eat with the weekly cooks and servers after the meal.

12. The brothers are not to read or sing in order, but only those who edify the listeners.

RB 39: THE QUANTITY OF FOOD

1. We believe that two cooked dishes are enough for the daily meal, whether at noon or mid-afternoon, at all times of the year. This is done because of the weaknesses of various persons, 2. for one who cannot eat one dish may be able to eat the other. 3. Therefore two cooked dishes should be enough for all the brothers, and if fruit or fresh vegetables are available, a third may be added. 4. A generous pound weight of bread should be enough for the day, whether it be for a single meal or for dinner and supper. 5. If they are to eat supper that day, a third part of the pound weight should be set aside by the cellarer for the evening meal.

6. If it should happen that the work has become especially heavy, the abbot may judge that something should be added. He has the power to do so if it seems useful, 7. provided above all that gluttony be avoided and the monk never be surprised by indigestion. 8. For there is nothing as out of place in a Christian life as gluttony. 9. As Our Lord says: *See that your hearts not be loaded down with drunkenness.*

10. The same amount of food, however, should not be served to young children, but less than to adults. Frugality should be maintained in all cases. 11. With the exception of those weak from illness, all the members must refrain from eating the flesh of four-footed animals.

RB 40: THE QUANTITY OF DRINK

1. *Each person is endowed by God with a special gift, some this, some that.* 2. Therefore it is with some uneasiness that we lay down rules for the consumption of others. 3. Nonetheless, keeping in view the weakness of the sick, we believe that an hemina of wine a day is sufficient for each one. 4. But those to whom God gives the strength to abstain from wine should know that they will have their own particular reward.

5. But if local circumstances or the workload or the heat of summer demand more, the superior has the power to grant it. But he should be constantly vigilant that excess and drunkenness do not creep in. 6. We read that wine is absolutely not for monks. But since monks in our day cannot be convinced of this, let us at least agree not to drink to excess, but sparingly. 7. *For wine makes even the wise go astray.*

8. When, though, local conditions are such that not even the amount mentioned above can be obtained, but much less or none at all, those who live there should bless God and not murmur. 9. Most of all we warn them to avoid murmuring.

Hospitality: Chapter 53

RB 53: THE RECEPTION OF GUESTS

1. All guests who arrive should be received as Christ, for he himself will say, *I was a stranger and you took me in.* 2. Proper respect should be shown to *all, especially fellow monks and pilgrims.*

3. So, as soon as a guest is announced, the superior or the brothers should hurry to meet him with every mark of love. 4. First they should pray together and then be united in peace. 5. The kiss of peace should not be given unless prayer has come first, on account of the wiles of the devil.

6. The greeting itself, however, ought to manifest complete humility toward guests who are arriving or departing: by an inclination of the head or by a complete prostration on the ground, one must adore Christ in them, for he is in fact the one who is received. 8. When they have been received, the guests should be led to prayer, and afterward the superior or his appointee should sit with them. 9. Let the Divine Law be read to the guest for edification, and after that he should be shown every sort of kindness.

10. The superior should break the fast on behalf of the guest, unless it be a principal fast day that cannot be violated. 11. The brothers, however, should keep the customary fasts. 12. The abbot should pour water on the hands of the guests. 13. The abbot as well as the whole congregation should wash the feet of all guests. 14. When they have been washed, let them pray this verse: *We have received, O God, your mercy in the midst of your temple.*

15. The greatest care should be exhibited in the reception of the poor and pilgrims, for Christ is more especially received in them; for the very fear of the rich wins them respect.

16. The kitchen of the abbot and the guests ought to be separate so that the guests, who are never in short supply in the monastery and who tend to arrive at odd hours, will not disturb the brothers. 17. Two brothers who can fulfill this task well should work in this kitchen for a year at a time. 18. Let help be given them as they need it so they may serve without complaint. On the other hand, when they have less to do, they should go out to work where they are assigned. 19. This principle pertains not only to them but to all officials in the monastery: 20. When they need help they should get it, but when they are unoccupied they should do what they are told.

21. A brother who is full of the fear of God should be assigned to the guest quarters. 22. A sufficient number of beds should be made up there. And the house of God should be wisely managed by wise persons.

23. Those who are not assigned to the guests are not to visit or speak with them. 24. But if one meets or sees guests, he should greet them humbly, as we said. One should ask for a blessing and then move on, explaining that it is not permitted to converse with a guest.

Administration of the Abbey: Chapters 64 and 66

RB 64: THE INSTALLATION OF THE ABBOT

1. In the installation of an abbot, the proper method is always to appoint the one whom the whole community agrees to choose in the fear of God. Or a part of the community, no matter how small, may make the choice if they possess sounder judgment. 2. Let the candidate be chosen for merit of life and wisdom of teaching, even if he hold the last rank in the community.

3. But it can happen that a whole community may conspire to choose a person who will go along with their vices—may it never happen! 4. If those goings-on somehow come to the notice of the local diocesan bishop, or to the abbots or Christians of the district, 5. they must block the evildoers from succeeding in their scheme. They should instead set a worthy steward over the house of God. 6. And they may be sure that they will receive a good reward for this deed if they have done it out of pure motives and godly zeal. But if they neglect their duty, they will be punished.

7. Once he has been installed, the abbot must constantly keep in mind what a burden he has undertaken and to whom he will have to *give a reckoning of his stewardship* (Luke 16:2). 8. And he should realize that he must profit others rather than precede them. 9. Therefore he must be learned in the Divine Law so he will know how to *bring forth things both old and new* (Matt 13:52). He should be chaste, temperate and merciful, 10. and always *put mercy before judgment* (Jas 2:13) so that he himself may obtain the former. 11. He should hate vices but love the brothers. 12. When he must correct someone, he should act prudently and *not overdo it*. If he is too vigorous in removing the rust, he may break the vessel. 13. Let him always be wary of his own brittleness, and remember not to break the bent reed. 14. We do not mean he should permit vices to flourish but that he should prune them with prudence and charity. As we said previously, he must use the method best suited to the individual. 15. He should aim more at being loved than feared. 16. He should not

be restless and troubled, not extreme and headstrong, not jealous and oversuspicious; for then he will have no peace. 17. In his commands he should be farsighted and thoughtful. And whether it is a question of spiritual or material matters, he should give prudent and moderate orders. 18. He should meditate on the prudence of holy Jacob, who said: *If I make my flock walk too far, they will all die in one day* (Gen 33:13). 19. Taking heed of these and other passages that extol discretion, the mother of virtues, he should arrange everything so that the strong are challenged and the feeble are not overwhelmed.

20. Most of all, he should keep to the present Rule in all things. 21. Then, when he has managed his office well, he will hear from the Lord what the good servant heard, who distributed grain to his fellow servants on time: 22. *Yes, I tell you,* he says *he sets him over his whole estate* (Matt 24:47).

RB 66: THE PORTERS OF THE MONASTERY

1. A wise old monk should be stationed at the gate of the monastery. He should know how to listen to people and also how to speak to them; his age should prevent him from wandering about. 2. The porter will need to have quarters near the gate so that those who arrive will always find him present to answer their call. 3. As soon as anyone knocks or a poor person cries out, he should respond "Thanks be to God!" or "Bless me!" 4. Filled with the gentleness of the fear of God, he must quickly respond in the warmth of charity. 5. If the porter needs help, he should be given a younger brother to assist him.

6. If possible, the monastery should be built so that all necessities such as water, mill and garden are contained within the walls so they can practice the various crafts there. 7. That way it will not be necessary for the monks to venture outside, for that is certainly not beneficial to their souls.

8. We want this Rule read rather often in the community so no brother can excuse himself because of ignorance.

The Final Chapter

RB 73: THAT THE WHOLE FULFILLMENT OF JUSTICE IS NOT LAID DOWN IN THIS RULE

1. We have sketched out this Rule, so that carrying it out in monasteries we may at least show that we have moral decency and the rudiments of a monastic life. 2. But for someone who is in a hurry to reach

the fullness of monastic life, there are the teachings of the Holy Fathers. Anyone who carries them out will arrive at the pinnacle of perfection. 3. For what page or even what word of the divinely inspired Old and New Testaments is not a completely reliable guidepost for human life? 4. Or what book of the holy Catholic Fathers does not teach us how to reach our Creator by the direct route? 5. And then there are the *Conferences* of the Fathers and their *Institutes* and *Lives*, along with the Rule of our holy Father Basil. 6. What else are they for monks who live upright and obedient lives but tools of virtue? 7. But for us lazy monks who lead bad and negligent lives, it is a source of embarrassment and shame.

8. Therefore, if you long to attain the heavenly homeland, with Christ's assistance carry out this modest Rule for beginners that we have sketched out. 9. Only then will you arrive with God's protection at the higher peaks of doctrine and virtue that we have pointed out. Amen.

Notes

Benedict (480–ca. 550) and Scholastica (480–ca. 547)

1. Now called Norcia and located in the Monti Sibillini National Park.

2. Remains of this early oratory, including frescoes, are located under the high altar of the Abbey Church of Monte Cassino. Nearby are the remains of Benedict and Scholastica. In all likelihood, some of their remains are still entombed at the Benedictine Monastery in Fleury, France.

3. *Gregory the Great: The Life of Saint Benedict*, trans. Hilary Costello and Eoin de Bhaldraithe with commentary by Adalbert de Vogüé (Petersham, MA: St. Bede's Press, 1993) 3.

4. Ibid., 154–55.

5. Ibid., 164.

6. Ibid., 174–75.

The Venerable Bede, Monk of Jarrow (ca. 673–735)

1. *Bede, Ecclesiastical History of the English People*. Trans. Leo Sherley-Price (New York: Penguin Classics, 1991) 336.

2. Ibid., 19–20.

3. Ibid.

4. Bede the Venerable, *Homilies on the Gospels. Book Two—Lent to the Dedication of the Church*. Trans. Lawrence T. Martin and David Hurst. (Kalamazoo: Cistercian Publications, 1991) 164–77.

Romuald of Ravenna (ca. 950–1027)

1. See Peter-Damian Belisle, "Primitive Romualdian/Camaldolese Spirituality," *Cistercian Studies Quarterly* 31:4 (1996), especially page 417.

2. Thomas Matus, *The Mystery of Romuald and the Five Brothers/Stories from the Benedictines & Camaldolese* (Trabuco Canyon, CA: Source Books, 1994) 66.

3. Peter Damian, *Life of St. Romuald of Ravenna*, trans. Henrietta Leyser in *Medieval Hagiography: an Anthology*, ed. Thomas Head (New York: Garland Publishing, 2000) 299–300.

4. Ibid., 303.

5. Ibid., 307–08.

6. Ibid., 311.

7. Ibid., 313–14.

Anselm of Canterbury (1033–1109)

1. William Shannon, *Anselm: the Joy of Faith* (New York: Crossroad Publishing, 1999) 15.

2. For example, see Hugh Feiss. *Essential Monastic Wisdom: Writings on the Contemplative Life* (HarperSanFrancisco, 1999) 191.

3. *The Prayers and Meditations of St. Anselm with the "Proslogion."* Trans. Benedicta Ward. (New York: Penguin, 1984) 89.

4. Shannon, 30.

5. Ibid., 182.

6. Ibid., 183.

7. *St. Anselm ~ Proslogium; Monologium; an Appendix in Behalf of the Fool by Gaunilon; and Cur Deus Homo*. Trans. Sidney Norton Deane (Chicago: Open Court Publishing, 1903) 3–7.

8. Ibid., 20–22.

9. Ibid., 33–34.

Hildegard of Bingen (1098–1179)

1. Hildegard of Bingen: *Scivias* as found in *Secrets of God: Writings of Hildegard of Bingen*, trans. Sabina Flanagan (Boston: Shambhala, 1996) 20–21.

2. Hildegard of Bingen: *Symphonia*, trans. Barbara Newman (Ithaca, NY: Cornell University Press) 151.

3. Ibid., 259.

4. Ibid., 101.

5. Ibid., 123.

Gertrud the Great of Helfta (1256–1302)

1. See the introduction to *Gertrude the Great: the Herald of Divine Love*. Trans. Margaret Winkworth (Mahwah, NJ: Paulist Press, 1992).

2. Miriam Schmitt, "Gertrud of Helfta: Her Monastic Milieu and Her Spirituality" in *Hidden Springs: Medieval Cistercian Women* (Kalamazoo: Cistercian Publications, 1995) 483.

3. *Gertrud the Great: The Herald of God's Loving-Kindness: Books I & 2*. Trans. Alexandra Barratt (Kalamazoo: Cistercian Publications, 1991) 100–108.

Dame Gertrude More (1606–1633)

1. The English realm, under the rule of King Henry the VIII and his successors comprised of present-day Great Britain or England, Scotland, Wales and Ireland.

2. Dame (in reference to women) and Dom (in reference to men) are titles given to English Benedictines, and the traditional way of addressing Benedictines.

3. The Counter-Reformation or the Catholic Reformation was the Catholic response to the Protestant Reformation. It culminated in the reforms of the Council of Trent.

4. *The Benedictines in Britain*, edited by D. H. Turner, Rachel Stockdale, Philip Jebb, and David Rogers (New York: Braziller, 1980) 94.

5. Dame Gertrude's term "Simplicitie" refers to union with God. "Multiplicitie" refers to unnecessary burdens that keep us from interior simplicity and hence an intimate relationship with God. "Aptness" is what comes naturally, in this case the contemplative's propensity toward imageless prayer.

6. The text is John 16:7 in Latin and can be translated: "If I do not go, the Paraclete will not come to you." Paraclete refers to the Holy Spirit.

7. Augustine Baker, O.S.B., *The Life and Death of Dame Gertrude More*, edited from all the known manuscripts by Ben Wekking (Salzburg, Austria: Analecta Cartusiana, 2002) 229–32.

8. The "directer" or "external maister" here is a spiritual director who would have been involved in guiding the sisters through Ignatian spiritual exercises, which Dame Gertrude speaks of here as not helpful to the contemplative soul.

9. Augustine Baker, O.S.B., *The Life and Death of Dame Gertrude More*, 245–46.

Blessed Columba Marmion (1858–1923)

1. See Translator's Introductory Note in *Christ, the Life of the Soul* by Blessed Columba Marmion, trans. Alan Bancroft, (Maryland: Zaccheus Press, Maryland) and (Gracewing Publishing), especially xix.

2. *Translator's note*: i.e. being in a state of grace at the time of death.

3. For instance, in a prayer prescribed for the feast-day of St. Prisca (January 18).

4. See Psalm 45 (46): 5.

5. See Ephesians 1:15-18.

6. See 1 Corinthians 2:10-12.

7. *Translator's note*: The judgment of each individual (the "particular judgment") takes place immediately on death, and this judgment determines the eternal destination of that soul: "it is appointed unto men once to die, and after this the judgment" (Heb 9:27). The Last Judgment—of everyone—will take place at the end of the world, at the coming of Christ in glory. It "will reveal even to its furthest consequences the good each person has done or failed to do during his earthly life": CCC, para. 1039. Preceding the Last Judgment, the mortal bodies of everyone will be brought to life again (Rom 8:11) and joined again to the individual souls ("the resurrection of the body"): CCC, paras. 998–1001.

8. *Translator's note*: Marmion uses this word, derived from the Latin *vita*, in the sense of "pertaining to life."

9. See Apocalypse 5:9-13.

10. Apocalypse 7:9.

11. III, q. XLV, a. 4.

12. "He predestined us to become conformed to the image of His Son": see Rom 8:29.

13. See 1 John 3:2.

14. See Colossians 3:9-10; cf. Ephesians 4:22-24.

15. According to St. Thomas (I-II, q. III, a. 4), beatitude consists essentially in the possession of God, gazed on face-to-face. This beatific vision is above all an act of the intellect; from this possession through the intellect there flows, as a property of it, beatitude of the will which finds its satisfaction and its repose in possession of the beloved object made present through the intellect.

16. See Apocalypse 7:12.

17. See Genesis 15:1.

18. St. Augustine, *Enarr. in Ps.* XLII, 2.

19. Matthew 25:21; Marmion alludes to words of Christ referring to it in parable.

20. *Epist. ad Honorat.* CXI, 31.
21. See Apocalypse 21:4.
22. See John 10:27-30.
23. See John 4:15.
24. Extract from Blessed Columba Marmion, O.S.B. *Christ, the Life of the Soul*, trans. Alan Bancroft (Maryland: Zaccheus Press [American edition], and Gracewing Publishing [U.K. edition], 2005).

Raïssa Maritain (1883–1960)

1. Raïssa Maritain. *We Have Been Friends Together* and *Adventures in Grace: the Memoirs of Raïssa Maritain*, trans. Julie Kernan. (New York: Image Books, 1961) 17.
2. Ibid., 33.
3. Ibid., 34.
4. Ibid., 39. At the time that Raïssa and Jacques were university students, *The Sorbonne* was the common name for the University of Paris.
5. Ibid., 67.
6. Ibid., 68.
7. Ibid., 85.
8. Ronda de Sola Chervin, *Prayers of the Women Mystics* (Ann Arbor, MI: Servant Publications, 1992) 210.
9. *We Have Been Friends Together*, 125.
10. *Raïssa's Journal, Presented by Jacques Maritain* (Albany, NY: Magi Books, 1974) 316–17.
11. Selections are from *Raïssa's Journal*, pages 29, 33, 40, 93, 125–26, 161, 164, 168, 229, 255, 275, 319, 328, 330, 381.

Bede Griffiths (1906–1993)

1. Bede Griffiths, *The Golden String* (Springfield, IL: Templegate Publishers, 1954/1980) 10.
2. Ibid., 78.
3. Ibid., 102.
4. Ibid., 108
5. Griffiths defines a *sanyasi* as one who has "renounced" the world, a word associated with Hindu mysticism. The sanyasi practices yoga, lives without possessions, and prays to God. The ultimate goal is to achieve enlightenment and liberation.
6. An ashram is a secluded religious community led by a guru. It is a tradition in India thousands of years old usually associated with Hinduism.
7. Bede Griffiths, *Return to the Center* (Springfield, IL: Templegate Publishers, 1994) 12.
8. Ibid., 16.
9. Beatrice Bruteau, "Prayer and Identity," *Contemplative Review*, 1983.
10. A reference to Adi Shankara also called *Bhagavatpada Acharya* (the teacher at the feet of the Lord) who lived around the 8th century. He had a profound influence on the growth of Hinduism. His teaching was non-dualistic and emphasized a spirituality based on reason without dogma or ritualism.
11. Bede Griffiths, *A New Vision of Reality: Western Science, Eastern Mysticism and Christian Faith*. Ed. Felicity Edwards (Springfield, IL: Templegate, 1990) 172–75.
12. Griffiths, *The Golden String*, 180–83.

Trappist Martyrs of Tibhirine, Algeria (d. 1996)

1. Bernardo Olivera. *How Far to Follow? The Martyrs of Atlas* (Petersham, MA: St. Bede's Publications, 1997) 17.

2. Ibid., 127.

3. Ibid., 34–35.

Benedictines and the Chant Tradition

1. See *The Grove Concise Dictionary of Music*, edited by Stanley Sadie (New York: W. W. Norton, 1994), especially the entry "Plainchant."

2. Early Christianity struggled to define its basic tenets and beliefs, and during the Third to Fifth Centuries also struggled to name who Jesus as Christ was for the Christian community (called the Christological Controversies), charges of heresy rung out. Often the charges were accurate, but not always. Since hymns serve to shape the believers understanding of the Christian faith, there was understandable concern that the texts be "true."

3. James McKinnon, "The Book of Psalms, Monasticism and the Western Liturgy" as in *The Place of the Psalms in the Intellectual Culture of the Middle Ages*, edited by Nancy Van Deusen (State University of New York Press, 1999) especially page 49.

4. See Laura Swan, *The Forgotten Desert Mothers: Lives, Sayings and Stories of Early Christian Women* (Mahwah, NJ: Paulist Press, 2001).

5. James McKinnon. *The Advent Project: the Later-Seventh-Century Creation of the Roman Mass Proper* (Berkeley: University of California Press, 2000) 375. "Extant" means surviving or existing. "Notated" means to write the text down. "Schola Cantorum" was the official choir and choir-school for St. Peter's at the Vatican, where the best vocalists were trained.

6. See Katharine Le Mée, *The Benedictine Gift to Music* (Mahwah, NJ: Paulist Press, 2003) 17.

7. Ibid., 13.

8. Prosper Guéranger, *Institutions liturgique*, vol. 3 (Paris: Julien, Lanier et Ce, Editeurs, 1851) 170–71. Trans. Michael Kwatera in *How Firm a Foundation: Leaders of the Liturgical Movement*, ed. By Robert Tuzik. Chicago: Liturgy Training Publications, 1990, page 17.

9. The nuns also faced expulsion at a later date and established a monastery at Ryde on the Isle of Wight. The nuns were eventually allowed to return and both monasteries flourish to this day.

10. Ibid., 55.

11. *How Firm a Foundation: Voices of the Early Liturgical Movement*. Compiled and Introduced by Kathleen Hughes. (Chicago: Liturgy Training Publications, 1990) 25.

12. Address of His Holiness Benedict XVI following a concert at the Sistine Chapel sponsored by the Domenico Bartolucci Foundation. *Vatican Information Services*. June 24, 2006. www.vatican.va/holy_father/benedict_xvi/speeches/2006/june/documents/hf_ben-xvi_spe_20060624_fondazione-bartolucci_en.html.

Conference of Benedictine Prioresses

1. Monastic chapter is the gathering of all perpetually professed members of a particular monastery. Any and all concerns of the monastery may be on the agenda for a chapter meeting. Monastic council is the formal body, elected or appointed, that

meets regularly with the prioress or abbot to conduct and oversee the important formal business of the monastery. The monastic council is shaped by canon law.

2. Conference of Benedictine Prioresses, *Wisdom from the Tradition: A Statement of North American Benedictine Women in Response to Our Times* (Atchison, KS: Privately Printed, 2006) 45–55.

Bibliography

The Benedictine Tradition

Barry, Patrick. *St. Benedict's Rule: a New Translation for Today*. Ampleforth Abbey/Hidden Spring, 2004.

Belisle, Peter-Damian, ed. *The Privilege of Love: Camaldolese Benedictine Spirituality*. Collegeville: Liturgical Press, 2002.

The Benedictine Handbook. Collegeville: Liturgical Press, 2003.

Casey, Michael. *Strangers to the City: Reflections on the Beliefs and Values of the Rule of Saint Benedict*. Brewster, MA: Paraclete Press, 2005.

Fry, Timothy, ed. *RB 1980: the Rule of St. Benedict in English: In Latin and English with Notes*. Collegeville: Liturgical Press, 1981.

Holzherr, George. *The Rule of Benedict: a Guide to Christian Living*. Dublin: Four Courts Press, 1994.

Kardong, Terrence. *Benedict's Rule: a Translation and Commentary*. Collegeville: Liturgical Press, 1996.

_____. *The Benedictines*. Wilmington, DE: Michael Glazier, 1988.

Powell, John. *Spiritual Teaching of the Brief Rule of Saint Romuald*. Big Sur: New Camaldoli Publications and Tapes, 1993.

Schmitt, Miriam and Linda Kulzer, eds. *Medieval Women Monastics: Wisdom's Wellsprings*. Collegeville: Liturgical Press, 1996.

Stewart, Columba. *Prayer and Community: the Benedictine Tradition*. Traditions of Christian Spirituality Series. Maryknoll, NY: Orbis Books, 1998.

Benedict (480–ca. 550) and Scholastica (480–ca. 547)

Butcher, Carmen Acevedo. *Man of Blessing: a Life of St. Benedict*. Brewster, MA: Paraclete Press, 2006.

Gregory the Great. *The Life of Saint Benedict*. Trans. Hilary Costello and Eoin de Bhaldraithe. Commentary by Adalbert de Vogüé. Petersham, MA: St. Bede's Publications, 1993.

The Venerable Bede, Monk of Jarrow (ca. 673–735)

Bede, Commentary on the Seven Catholic Epistles. Trans. David Hurst. Kalamazoo: Cistercian Publications, 1985.

Bede, Ecclesiastical History of the English People. Intro. David H. Farmer, Ronald E. Latham, Trans. Leo Sherley-Price. New York: Penguin Classics, 1991.

Bede's Ecclesiastical History of the English People: A Historical Commentary. Ed. J. M. Wallace-Hadril. Oxford Medieval Texts. Oxford University Press, 1993.

The Venerable Bede: Commentary on the Acts of the Apostles. Trans. Lawrence T. Martin. Kalamazoo: Cistercian Publications, 1989.

_____. *Homilies on the Gospels. Book One—Advent to Lent*. Trans. Lawrence T. Martin and David Hurst. Kalamazoo: Cistercian Publications, 1991.

_____. *Homilies on the Gospels. Book Two—Lent to the Dedication of the Church*. Trans. Lawrence T. Martin and David Hurst. Kalamazoo: Cistercian Publications, 1991.

Romuald of Ravenna (ca. 950–1027)

Bruno-Boniface of Querfurt, Saint. *The Life of the Five Brothers*. Trans. Thomas Matus, in *The Mystery of Romuald and the Five Brothers*. Big Sur: Source Books/Hermitage Books, 1994.

Peter Damian. *Life of St. Romuald of Ravenna*. Trans. Henrietta Leyser, in *Medieval Hagiography: an Anthology*, Ed. Thomas Head. New York: Garland Publishing, 2000.

Anselm of Canterbury (1033–1109)

Anselm of Canterbury: the Major Works. Ed. Brian Davies and G. R. Evans. Oxford University Press, 1998.

Fröhlich, Walter, ed. *The Letters of St. Anselm of Canterbury*. Kalamazoo: Cistercian Publications, vol. 1, 1990; vol. 2, 1993; vol. 3, 1994.

Prayers and Meditations of St. Anselm with the "Proslogion." Trans. Benedicta Ward. London: Penguin, 1973. Harmondsworth, 1979.

Shannon, William. *Anselm: the Joy of Faith*. The Crossroad Spiritual Legacy Series. New York: Crossroad Publishing Company, 1997.

St. Anselm. *Proslogium; Monologium; an Appendix in Behalf of the Fool by Gaunilon; and Cur Deus Homo*. Trans. Sidney Norton Deane. Chicago: Open Court Publishing, 1903.

Ward, Benedicta. *Anselm of Canterbury: a Monastic Scholar*. Kalamazoo: Cistercian Publications, 1973.

Bernard of Clairvaux (1090–1153)

Bernard of Clairvaux: Five Books on Consideration: Advice to a Pope. Trans. John Anderson and Elizabeth T. Kennan. Kalamazoo: Cistercian Publications, 1976.

Bernard of Clairvaux: Homilies in Praise of the Blessed Virgin Mary. Trans. Marie-Bernard Saïd. Kalamazoo: Cistercian Publications, 1993.

Bernard of Clairvaux: The Life and Death of Saint Malachy the Irishman. Trans. Robert T. Meyer. Kalamazoo: Cistercian Publications, 1978.

Bernard of Clairvaux: On Baptism and the Office of Bishops. Trans. Pauline Matarasso. Kalamazoo: Cistercian Publications, 2005.

Bernard of Clairvaux: On Grace and Free Choice. Trans. Daniel O'Donovan. Kalamazoo: Cistercian Publications, 1988.

Bernard of Clairvaux: On Loving God. Trans. Robert Walton. Kalamazoo: Cistercian Publications, 1995.

Bernard of Clairvaux: The Parables and the Sentences. Trans. Michael Casey and Francis R. Swietek. Kalamazoo: Cistercian Publications, 1993.

Bernard of Clairvaux: Selected Works. Trans. G. R. Evans. Classics of Western Spirituality Series. Mahwah, NJ: Paulist Press, 1987.

Bernard of Clairvaux: Sermons for the Summer Season. Trans. Beverly Kienzle with James Jarzembowski. Kalamazoo: Cistercian Publications, 1991.

Bernard of Clairvaux: Sermons on Conversion. Trans. Marie Bernard Saïd. Kalamazoo: Cistercian Publications, 1981.

Bernard of Clairvaux: Sermons on the Song of Songs. Trans. Kilian Walsh and Irene Edmonds. 4 vols. Kalamazoo: Cistercian Publications, 1971; 1976; 1979; 1980.

Bernard of Clairvaux: the Steps of Humility and Pride. Kalamazoo: Cistercian Publications, 1989.

Cistercians and Cluniacs: Bernard of Clairvaux's Apologia to Abbot William. Trans. Michael Casey. Kalamazoo: Cistercian Publications, 1970.

Hildegard of Bingen (1098–1179)

Hildegard of Bingen: Mystical Writings. Eds. Fiona Bowie and Oliver Davies. Trans. Robert Carver. New York: Crossroad Press, 1990.

Hildegard of Bingen. *Explanation of the Rule of Benedict*. Trans. Hugh Feiss. Toronto: Peregrina Press, 1990.

_____. *Play of the Virtues*. Trans. Peter Dronke as found in *Nine Medieval Latin Plays*. Cambridge: Cambridge University Press, 1994.

_____. *Scivias*. Trans. Columba Hart and Jane Bishop. Classics of Western Spirituality Series. New York: Paulist Press, 1990.

_____. *Symphonia: a Critical Edition of the Symphonia Armonie Celestium Revelationum*. Trans. Barbara Newman. Ithaca: Cornell University Press, 1989.

Jutta & Hildegard: the Biographical Sources. Trans. Anna Silvas. University Park, PA: Penn State University Press, 1998.

Letters of Hildegard of Bingen. Trans. Joseph Baird and Radd Ehrman. Oxford: Oxford University Press, 1994, 1998.

Life of the Saintly Hildegard. Trans. Hugh Feiss. Toronto: Peregrina Press, 1996.

Secrets of God: Writings of Hildegard of Bingen. Trans. Sabina Flanagan. Boston: Shambhala, 1996.

Gertrud the Great of Helfta (1256–1302)

Gertrud the Great of Helfta: Spiritual Exercises. Trans. Gertrud Jaron Lewis and Jack Lewis. Kalamazoo: Cistercian Publications, 1989.

Gertrud the Great: The Herald of God's Loving-Kindness–Books 1 & 2. Trans. Alexandra Barratt. Kalamazoo: Cistercian Publications, 1991.

Gertrud the Great: The Herald of God's Loving-Kindness–Book 3. Trans. Alexandra Barratt. Kalamazoo: Cistercian Publications, 2006.

Gertrude the Great: the Herald of Divine Love. Trans. Margaret Winkworth. The Classics of Western Spirituality Series. Mahwah, NJ: Paulist Press, 1992.

Dame Gertrude More (1606–1633)

Baker, Augustine. *The Inner Life and Writings of Dame Gertrude More*, Ed. Dom Benedict Weld-Brundell. London: R. T. Washbourne Ltd, 1910–1911.

Sandeman, Dame Frideswide. *Dame Gertrude More*. United Kingdom: Gracewing, 1997.

Wekking, Ben, ed. *Augustine Baker O.S.B. The Life and Death of Dame Gertrude More*. Salzburg: Analecta Cartusiana, 2003.

Blessed Columba Marmion (1858–1923)

Marmion, Blessed Columba. *Christ in His Mysteries: Spiritual and Liturgical Conferences*. Trans. nun of Tyburn convent. St. Louis, MO: Herder, 1924.

_____. *Christ the Ideal of the Monk: Spiritual Conferences on the Monastic and Religious Life*. Trans. nun of Tyburn convent. St. Louis, MO: B. Herder, 1926.

_____. *Christ, the Life of the Soul: Spiritual Conferences*. Trans. Alan Bancroft. Bethesda, MD: Zaccheus Press, 2005.

_____. *The English Letters of Abbot Marmion, 1858–1923*. Baltimore, MD: Helicon Press, 1962.

_____. *Union with God, according to the Letters of Direction of Dom Marmion*. Ed. Dom Raymond, Trans. Mother Mary St. Thomas. London: Sands & Co. [1949, c1934]. Reprint forthcoming from Zaccheus Press, 2006.

_____. *The Way of the Cross: Its Efficacy and Practice*. Trans. nun of Tyburn convent. St. Louis, MO: B. Herder, 1960. Reprinted 1997, available from Marmion Abbey, IL 60504.

Tierney, Mark, O.S.B. *Dom Columba Marmion: a Biography*. Dublin: Columba Press, 1994.

Raïssa Maritain (1883–1960)

Barré, Jean-Luc, *Jacques and Raïssa Maritain: Beggars for Heaven*. South Bend, IN:University of Notre Dame Press, 2005.

Exiles and Fugitives: the Letters of Jacques and Raïssa Maritain, Allen Tate, and Caroline Gordon. Ed. John M. Dunaway. Baton Rouge, LA: Louisiana State University Press, 1992.

Maritain, Raïssa. *We Have Been Friends Together* and *Adventures in Grace. The Memoirs of Raïssa Maritain*. New York: Image Books, 1961.

_____. *Raïssa's Journal, Presented by Jacques Maritain*. Albany, NY: Magi Books, 1974.

Suther, Judith D. *Raïssa Maritain: Pilgrim, Poet, Exile*. New York: Fordham University Press, 1990.

Bede Griffiths (1906–1993)

Bede Griffiths: Essential Writings. Ed. Thomas Matus. Modern Spiritual Masters Series. Maryknoll, NY: Orbis Books, 2004.

Griffiths, Bede. *Bede Griffiths*. Modern Spirituality Series. Springfield, IL: Templegate, 1993.

_____. *Christ in India: Essays towards a Christian-Hindu Dialogue*. Springfield, IL: Templegate, 1994.

_____. *Christianity in the Light of the East*. Hibbert Trust. London, 1989.

_____. *The Cosmic Revelation: The Hindu Way to God*. Springfield, IL: Templegate, 1994.

_____. *The Golden String; an Autobiography*. Springfield, IL: Templegate, 1992.

_____. *Marriage of East and West: a Sequel to the Golden String*. Springfield, IL: Templegate, 1992.

_____. *A New Vision of Reality: Western Science, Eastern Mysticism, and Christian Faith*. Springfield, IL: Templegate, 1992.

_____. *Return to the Center*. Springfield, IL: Templegate, 1994.

_____. *River of Compassion: A Christian Commentary on the Bhagavad Gita*. New York: Continuum, 1987.

_____. *Universal Wisdom: A Journey through the Sacred Wisdom of the World.* New York: HarperCollins. 1994.

Swindells, John, ed. *A Human Search. Bede Griffiths Reflects on His Life*. Triumph Books. 1997.

Trappist Martyrs of Tibhirine (d. 1996)

Kiser, John W. *The Monks of Tibhirine: Faith, Love and Terror in Algeria*. New York: St. Martins Press, 2002.

Olivera, Bernado. *How Far to Follow? The Martyrs of Atlas*. Petersham, MA: St. Bede's Publications, 1997.

Chant Tradition

Hiley, David. *Western Plainchant: A Handbook*. New York: Oxford University Press, 1995.

Le Mée, Katharine. *The Benedictine Gift to Music*. Mahwah, NJ: Paulist Press, 2003.

McKinnon, James. *The Advent Project: the Later-Seventh-Century Creation of the Roman Mass Proper*. University of California Press, 2000.

Moorhead, John. *Gregory the Great*. Early Church Fathers series. Routledge, 2005.

Pecklers, Keith. *The Unread Vision: The Liturgical Movement in the United States of America: 1926–1955*. Collegeville: Liturgical Press, 1998.

The Spirit of Solesmes: The Christian Life in the Works of Dom Prosper Guéranger, Abbess Cécile Bruyèr, Dom Paul Delatte. Ed. Sister Mary David Totah. Petersham, MA: St. Bede's Publications, 1997.

How Firm a Foundation: Leaders of the Liturgical Movement, Ed. Robert Tuzik. Chicago: Liturgy Training Publications, 1990.

How Firm a Foundation: Voices of the Early Liturgical Movement. Compiled and Introduced by Kathleen Hughes. Chicago: Liturgy Training Publications, 1990.

Conference of Benedictine Prioresses

Upon This Tradition: Five Statements on Monastic Values in the Lives of American Benedictine Sisters. Reprinted with Prologues and Updates. Privately Printed by the Conference of American Benedictine Prioresses, 2001.

Wisdom from the Tradition: A Statement of North American Benedictine Women in Response to Our Times. Privately Printed by the Conference of American Benedictine Prioresses, Atchison, KS, 2006.